To michael & Sh

Best regards.

Ian & Sharon

# The Murder That Never Dies

By Eudon Holland and Laurie A. Palazzolo

FERNE PRESS

**The Murder That Never Dies**
Copyright © 2013 by Eudon Holland and Laurie A. Palazzolo
Layout and cover design by Jacqueline L. Challiss Hill

Printed in the United States

Summary: A probing look into several unsolved murders in Slocomb, Alabama.

**Library of Congress Cataloging-in-Publication Data**
Holland, Eudon and Palazzolo, Laurie A.
The Murder That Never Dies/Eudon Holland and Laurie A. Palazzolo–
First Edition
ISBN-13: 978-1-938326-04-2
1. Non-fiction. 2. Alabama. 3. Unsolved murders.
I. Holland, Eudon and Palazzolo, Laurie A. II. Title.
Library of Congress Control Number: 2012943332

The views and opinions expressed by the authors are theirs alone and are not representative of the views and opinions of the publisher.

FERNE PRESS

Ferne Press is an imprint of Nelson Publishing & Marketing
366 Welch Road, Northville, MI 48167
www.nelsonpublishingandmarketing.com
(248) 735-0418

# Table of Contents

Front Cover Photo: Gordon Wright Smith, M.D. (ca. 1920)

Back Cover Photos: Gordon Wright Smith, M.D.'s mansion in Slocomb,
Alabama, Grave site of Gordon Wright Smith, M.D., Grave site of Alice Dixie
Whitaker Smith ("Aunt Dixie"), Wife of Gordon W. Smith, M.D.

# SMITH-WHITAKER FAMILY TREE

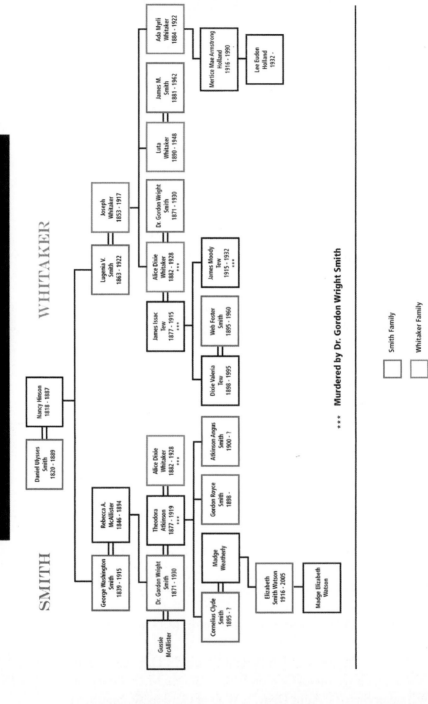

**SMITH**

**WHITAKER**

Daniel Ulysses Smith
1820 - 1889

Nancy Hinson
1818 - 1887

Rebecca A. McAllister
1846 - 1894

George Washington Smith
1839 - 1915

Lugenia V. Smith
1863 - 1922

Joseph Whitaker
1853 - 1917

Ada Myrti Whitaker
1884 - 1922

James M. Smith
1881 - 1962

Luta Whitaker
1890 - 1948

Dr. Gordon Wright Smith
1871 - 1930

Alice Dixie Whitaker
1882 - 1928 ***

Mertice Mae Armstrong Holland
1916 - 1990

Lee Eudon Holland
1932 -

James Issac Tew
1877 - 1915 ***

James Moody Tew
1915 - 1932 ***

Web Foster Smith
1895 - 1960

Dixie Valeria Tew
1898 - 1995

Theodora Atkinson
1877 - 1919 ***

Alice Dixie Whitaker
1882 - 1928 ***

Atkinson Angus Smith
1900 - ?

Dr. Gordon Wright Smith
1871 - 1930

Gordon Royce Smith
1898 -

Gussie McAllister

Cornelius Clyde Smith
1895 - ?

Madge Weatherly

Elizabeth Smith Watson
1916 - 2005

Madge Elizabeth Watson

*** **Murdered by Dr. Gordon Wright Smith**

☐ Smith Family

☐ Whitaker Family

# Acknowledgments

This book would not have been possible without the contributions of many dedicated and generous people. Among them are Tony Kelly and Billy Newton, who provided invaluable historical information regarding Dr. Smith and the Slocomb and Geneva County areas and greatly assisted me in attempting to present the events as they actually happened. Also to Max Kelly, who guided me to them, and to the many members of his Slocomb High School Class of 1951 who contributed to this book. They all were an inspiration to me.

I'm very grateful to Sharon Dombrowski, my dear friend and companion, for her many contributions and support throughout the writing of the book.

I'm also grateful to Jennifer Walker for her technical support, assistance, and loyalty throughout the writing of this book.

James and Dorothy Coe provided photographs of the grave sites of Dr. Smith and Aunt Dixie and guided and assisted me in many other ways.

To Jo Holmes I am deeply indebted, as without her *My Home Town: A History of Slocomb, Alabama: 1901–2001* and "The Knife," this book would not have been nearly as complete. They were the inspiration for my starting the book after wishing to do so for many years.

I'm grateful to Martha (Cook) Smith for providing the Smith genealogy.

Tillie Van Sickle provided genealogical information on the Smith and Whitaker families and photographs of the grave site of Isaac Tew and was helpful in so many other ways.

I'm grateful to Wynton Melton, mayor of Geneva, Alabama, for all his efforts in providing resource people.

Rhonda Stan provided the cover photographs of Dr. Smith and his mansion, for which I'm most grateful.

Cliff Knight, a minister of students at Auburn University and a descendant of the Whitaker family, provided a copy of the newspaper article on the death of Moody Tew and information on the Whitaker family.

To Lon Everett and James Earl Best, Jr., who wrote *From Holme to Holmes: The Saga of the Whitaker Family in America*, I'm deeply indebted.

To all of these individuals, and to all those not mentioned here who helped in ways that are not expressed but whose efforts are nonetheless as important, I express my heartfelt gratitude.

Written in Honor of My Mother,
Mertice Mae (Armstrong) Holland,
and Her Mother, Ada Myrli (Whitaker) Armstrong

This story is based upon what the writers have been told by, and what we have read in, our sources. We have attempted in all cases to be as accurate as possible. However, the information we received was taken from different accounts written and told by different individuals. Therefore, where conflicts or discrepancies exist, it is due to the fact that individual recollections or accounts may vary.

# Introduction

Some things stay with you for the rest of your life. Like the story of a murder told to you by your mother. Like a murder that refuses to die.

I was just a child back in the 1930s when my mother began telling me the story of several murders that were committed in Slocomb, Alabama, back in her childhood. My mother and her sister, my Aunt Myrtelee, would repeat the story over and over again to me when I was a child. It was a common topic of conversation at family gatherings. One of the murders was particularly prominent and gruesome, and it lives on to this day.

There were accomplices in that most famous of murders. My mother vividly remembered when the trial was being held. She was only twelve years old and was living with her father and stepmother, Idella, in Eunola, Alabama, in Geneva County, four miles from Geneva and fifteen miles from Slocomb. She remembered seeing her cousin drive past her house every day from his home in Slocomb on his way to the courthouse in Geneva to watch the trial.

Years later, on the winter afternoon of December 26, 1987, I was interviewing my mother to gather our family's history, a project that had been entrusted to me by my Aunt Myrtelee. I never expected that the murder would once again creep up, probing its way into my conscience again like the tip of an iceberg, calling me to investigate the glacier of other murders that allegedly had been committed so coldly and calculatingly by the same perpetrator back in the steamy South during the 1920s.

What my mother said on that bleak winter afternoon would continue to haunt me for over twenty years. I seemed to know that I would return one day to explore the murders—that I would have to put to rest the mysteries that were never resolved.

It's as though I had an inner voice that told me I had to write this story. Or, maybe, from heaven my mom was driving me to write the book. I believe she was the force behind my writing our joint memoir, *Boiled Peanuts and Buckeyes*.

I felt that my writing this story would further keep my mom's memory and spirit alive. Also, it would answer many questions for people in the Slocomb community. In addition, there were other related deaths that I felt needed to be brought to light.

After I finished my and my mother's memoirs and when I first set out on this journey, I thought I would encounter resistance based on stories I had heard from people in Slocomb. For decades, no one in Slocomb or Geneva County would talk openly about the most famous murder. The subject was taboo—forbidden. It was a common belief around those parts that someone might want you dead if you talked about it. When I began writing my family history, I discovered some history about it. Many years later, I began to dig seriously into the research, and I traveled from my home in Michigan down to Slocomb and Geneva, as well as to Bonifay, Florida, on a few occasions. I uncovered newspaper articles relating details of the case and the trial, as well as a well-known article published in a detective magazine, *True Detective Mysteries*.

I spoke to people who were familiar with the murder, including one lifelong Slocomb resident who revealed that for years no one knew the reason why the murder had happened, and they did not know the reason until I shared the information with them. She said that her father was so terrified to talk about it that he refused to do so, claiming that someone might want him dead. He had a copy of the magazine article, which he kept between the mattresses of his bed. He told his children that they could read it but that they were not to talk about it.

But surprisingly, I found little resistance from the people I met and talked to in Slocomb as I began to write my account of the case, even those who were friends of descendants of the alleged perpetrator.

The people with whom I talked and the articles that I discovered revealed that Alabama attorney general Charles F. McCall himself directed the investigation, and he himself prosecuted the case. This was standard procedure back then, but as a result of the way the case was tried and its outcome, and as a result of other cases, the process changed afterward.

The case had such an incredibly unbelievable outcome that it sent a shock wave through Slocomb and Geneva County, Alabama, that would continue to reverberate in the decades to come. Many could not believe and still cannot believe that all this could happen in the sleepy little town of Slocomb.

# Chapter 1

## Slocomb, Alabama
### A Town of Morals and Family Values

Slocomb, Alabama, in Geneva County, is part of the Wiregrass Region, which encompasses nine counties and stretches along the Choctawhatchee and Pea rivers. The region derives its name from the native forest plant that covers the area, shooting up out of the earth like long, emerald-colored strands of wire. At one time Spanish, and then British, cattle herders were attracted to the area because of the food that the wiregrass provided for their large herds of cattle. Later, early American settlers used the plant for cattle grazing (Era Jo Harris Holmes, *My Home Town: A History of Slocomb, Alabama: 1901–2001*).

Slocomb, back in the 1920s, was a town that has been described as being a lot like Mayberry of the popular 1960s sitcom *Mayberry R.F.D.* It was a town where little girls proudly walked to school and church in their dresses that their mothers made by hand out of flowered flour sacks (Harris Holmes).

Dalton's Drug Store was a local mainstay. That was where you went to purchase penny candy or an RC Cola, in addition to pharmaceuticals. While you sat and sipped on a milkshake, Slocomb's five doctors—yes, five, in a town of about 2,400—smiled down upon you from framed photographs hanging on the wall above the soda fountain.

Many doctors started out with their offices in the back of a drugstore. The first doc-

Dr. D. D. Stephens:
Mayor 1928-1944, Author of "The Knife".

1

tors in the city included Drs. C. C. Dalton, G. H. Herring, Mordecai E. Doughty, John Chalker, G. W. Smith (the subject of this book), D. D. Stephens (also the mayor intermittently for several years), and D. B. O'Kelley. In 1905, Dr. C. C. Dalton had his office in Dalton's Drug Store. Slocomb and Dalton's Drug Store were proud of their doctors, who delivered babies, made house calls carrying their little black bags filled with surgical instruments and tinctures, and cared for Slocomb's mothers, fathers, and children (Harris Holmes).

Saturday was the big day when everyone in this farming community piled into the family vehicle—which most often was a mule-drawn wagon, since most people didn't have automobiles then—and drove into town. The general store was filled with women doing their weekly shopping. It was where everyone went for groceries and the myriad dry goods that were essential for day-to-day living, such as textiles, oilcloth, pottery, utensils, notions, clothing, hats, shoes, groceries, hardware, farming items, furniture, and even coffins.

In fact, in the early days of Slocomb, you could even purchase laudanum over the counter in stores. Laudanum, also known as tincture of opium, is an alcoholic herbal preparation containing approximately 10 percent powdered opium (the equivalent of 1 percent morphine). It is a potent narcotic and originally was used as a cough suppressant and as an analgesic. It could be purchased in stores in Slocomb in the days prior to 1930, when Slocomb was still a "wet" town. Slocomb and Geneva County went "dry" in 1930, when the populace voted for prohibition on the sale of alcohol in the community, and the prohibition remained until November 2010 (Harris Holmes).

Before prohibition, the state controlled the distribution of alcohol. During the 1920s, there was a hotel in Slocomb that had a saloon where alcohol was sold. The State of Alabama allotted a certain percentage of alcohol per town based upon population, and it was shipped by rail in barrels. Some enterprising person figured out how to access the whiskey by boring a hole through the barrels and one day stole all the whiskey by siphoning it out of the barrels. The town of Slocomb went "dry" until the arrival of the next load of whiskey.

Dwight Tew, retired teacher and football coach at Slocomb High School, who provided me with the above story, heard it from policeman Ernest A. Davis. Dwight graduated from Slocomb High School in 1963. Elizabeth Masters, Dr. Smith's great-granddaughter, taught him mathematics at Slocomb High School.

While the women shopped in Slocomb, the men caught up on the latest news with one another. The main street was like a scene from a magazine with men leaning against buildings as they chewed tobacco, dipped snuff, or smoked pipes or cigarettes. Folks greeted one another as they walked through town; men tipped their hats and ladies smiled and waved hello. Strolling down the main street on a Saturday afternoon, you were sure to see and hear a young boy chanting his sales pitch while peddling homemade boiled peanuts from a shoebox:

> *Fresh boiled peanuts, five cents a bag;*
> *Fresh and fine, right off the vine.*
> *If you don't have a nickel,*
> *I can change a dime!*

Peddlers came into Slocomb with the beds of their wagons overflowing with goods, which they hoped to sell and then return home having made a good profit. When left unattended, those wares were as safe on the street as one of Aunt Bee's apple pies that she baked for Andy and Opie, cooling out on the open windowsill of the family home in *Mayberry R.F.D.* It was a self-perpetuating world, with people living off the land and taking care of their families and of one another (Harris Holmes).

Folks in Slocomb back in the 1920s made do with what they had. They were hard-working, imaginative, and resourceful. The days of public, tiled, in-ground swimming pools filled with aqua filtered and bleached water were a vision of the future. When you were hot, you walked down to the local creek and jumped in. When you got a sore throat, you didn't run to the doctor, although Slocomb did revere its numerous medical professionals. You simply relied on Mom to conjure up a mixture of mineral oil and sugar or kerosene and sugar as a tonic. And when you scraped your knee playing hopscotch, Blind Man's Bluff, Cowboys and Indians, or Cops and Robbers, Mom soothed it by whipping up a mixture of kerosene and iodine. Most people did not run to the doctor for minor ailments. When you really did need a doctor, one of those five Slocomb physicians would make a house call (Harris Holmes).

It was also a small melting pot, as the area was a settling place for Russian Jews during this period that saw a huge influx of these immigrants following the Russian Revolution (Tony Kelly, telephone conversation with the authors, March 11, 2011).

Although the lumber business was a mainstay at this time in Slocomb, back in the late 1800s it was the turpentine industry that had kept Slocomb's economy strong due to the area's abundance of pine forests. It was Frank Slocomb and his brother Will, settlers of Slocomb, who had set up the first turpentine still about two miles from town in 1898. Back then, in addition to turpentine, cross ties and lumber were among Slocomb's early industries. According to William Rigell of Johnson City, Tennessee, who wrote a history of the town, the Slocomb brothers controlled the turpentine business, "Doc" Anthony headed up the cross tie busi-

3

ness, and the Morris Lumber Company ran the sawmill (http://genevaareacham-ber.com/Cities/Slocomb/tabid/418/Default.aspx).

"Doc" Anthony is described as a delightful citizen of Slocomb. He felled much of the pine and cypress before the timber was sent to the Morris Lumber Company for processing. From there, the finished product was shipped to many parts of the world (Harris Holmes).

The Morris Lumber Company, or the mill, was later operated by, among others, G. S. (Sumpter) Kelley, Henry (Daniel) Clark, and J. C. Ausley. It was located across the Graceville (Florida) Highway in an area that later became the machine shop of Cornelius Smith (Dr. Smith's son, more commonly known as Clyde Smith). It originally was established to cut ties for the modern railroad. Not only did the Morris Lumber Company become the backbone of Slocomb's economy, employing approximately one thousand men, but the lumber that it put out also became known throughout the world. Homeowners throughout Slocomb were proud of the lumber that went into their homes, which contained no knots whatsoever. Oxen were kept in a barn behind the lumber company and were maintained by Henry Fullford. He also put the oxen to work to haul the timber for the lumber company. Four or six yokes of oxen hauled log carts containing the timber that had been cut by crosscut saws. The timber was also pulled by a locomotive engineered by Otis Brownlow and fired by Cleve Ethridge, run on the Central of Georgia main line (Harris Holmes).

After the Morris Lumber Company went out of business, Raymond Weatherly and Clyde Smith purchased and operated a lumber company at the location for many years. Clyde Smith owned and operated his machine shop at the location for several more years after the lumber company closed (Harris Holmes).

Many other sawmills were built. Another important lumber company in the Slocomb area was the Kelly-Clark on Pate Creek (Harris Holmes).

As the pines were cleared, the land was used to grow cotton, corn, and peanuts. Cotton became the economy's chief staple. When cotton became the predominant industry, thousands—blacks and whites alike—turned to the fields for their livelihood. The grueling work of cotton picking could not be done for very long without knee pads to minimize the impact of the weight of the body on the knees and to keep from bearing down on twigs and stones as one crawled along in the fields picking the cotton under the scorching hot sun. A long cotton sack was strewn across one shoulder, strapped on, and hung under the other arm. Workers were paid according to the weight of cotton picked and turned in at the end of each day (Harris Holmes).

There were many "cotton houses" in the fields. These were small buildings where the cotton was delivered after it was picked and before it was delivered to the cotton gin. After the cotton approached the weight sufficient for a ginned bale, it was loaded onto a wagon and delivered to one of Slocomb's many gins for ginning. There were at least five gins in Slocomb. Four gins that were operating in the early days of Slocomb were the Faircloth-Segrest Gin, which later became the Segrest Gin; the Farm Bureau Gin owned by Tully Weeks; the Charles Carmichael Smith (apparently no relation to Dr. Smith) Gin; and a gin owned by Ed Watford (Harris Holmes).

The Segrest family was prominent in industry in Slocomb and also owned Segrest Feed & Seed Company, Faircloth Segrest Mercantile, Segrest Warehouse, and Faircloth Segrest Stables. Mr. C. E. Segrest later became president of Slocomb National Bank (Harris Holmes).

Another prominent family in business in Slocomb was the Harris family. Prominent and familiar businesses were the Harris Bros. Warehouse and Harris Bros. General Merchandise, which became Harris Bros. Grocery and then Harris Bros. Hardware (Harris Holmes).

Once the cotton was delivered to the gins, the machines separated the cotton fibers from the seeds. This previously was done by hand, before Eli Whitney's invention of the cotton gin in the late 1700s.

Beginning in the 1920s, most people farmed and picked cotton for a living. Today, tomatoes and truck farming are Slocomb's main sources of industry (Harris Holmes).

Like most southern towns, Slocomb was a God-fearing and God-worshipping place. On Sunday morning, church bells rang out from the bell towers of nearly a dozen churches. Each Saturday afternoon, the loud voice of a preacher could be heard bellowing the gospel from a sidewalk in town as passersby went about their business. It was a place where the steps of the Slocomb National Bank served as a temporary police station, where Ernest A. Davis, the only policeman in town, perched himself and kept "watch" over the place, even though things rarely got out of hand in this town of unlocked doors (Harris Holmes).

Slocomb was a place where you didn't have to worry about crime, a place where "a man's word was his bond and it was sealed with a handshake." It was a safe place, a place where you only read in the newspaper about the bad things that happened in the world (Harris Holmes).

But every city and every family has its secrets, and as the Bible says, the day will come when "nothing that is concealed will not be disclosed or hidden that will not be made known; what you have said in the dark will be heard in the daylight, and what you have whispered in the ear in the inner rooms will be proclaimed from the roofs." And in reading this story, it is just as important to remember that the corner preacher in Slocomb during the time also would undoubtedly have been reminding passersby of Romans 3:23: *"For all have sinned and fall short of the glory of God"* (Luke 12:2–3 [NIV]; Romans 3:23 [NIV]).

# Chapter 2

## A Tale of Two Families Related by Marriage:
### The Whitakers and the Smiths

The pages of fictional and nonfictional history alike are filled with stories of famous, prominent, and tragic families. Not to be outdone, Slocomb had the Smiths, and Geneva County had the Whitakers. These two families historically certainly rank among the most prominent in Slocomb and Geneva County at the time, and the Smiths perhaps to this day—and they do create their own unique aura of tragedy. In addition, there were intermarriages between the two families.

According to documented research, my mother's mother, Ada Myrli (Whitaker) Armstrong, was a direct descendant of the Whitakers of England, who are descended from William the Conqueror—the illegitimate warrior-conqueror King of England—through Mary Bourchier, wife of Jabez Whitaker (1595–1626). This long line of clergy and nobles of the time—as many as eight generations of Whitakers—are buried at a church in Holme, England (Lon Everett and James Earl Best, Jr., *From Holme to Holmes: The Saga of the Whitaker Family in America* [Dothan, AL: Minuteman Press, 1991]; Lee Eudon Holland, Laurie A. Palazzolo, and Danny Kanat, *Boiled Peanuts and Buckeyes* [Northville, MI: Ferne Press, 2006]).

Grave site of Ada Myrli (Whitaker) Armstrong (my grandmother).

The Whitakers of England were a very influential and wealthy family. William began conquering kingdoms at the age of twenty, along with Henry, King of France.

William became the most powerful duke in the province of Maine and the mightiest dependent landholder of the French Crown, and he was also known as a great diplomat. He married Matilda, daughter of the Earl of Flanders, in 1053. In perhaps what was his greatest military feat, he conquered England in 1066. His legacy lives on in the form of today's English government (Everett and Best; Holland, Palazzolo, and Kanat).

Eventually the Whitakers immigrated to America. Reverend Alexander Whitaker, who was born in 1585, distinguished himself greatly and is mentioned in many history books. He was left fatherless in the world, being only ten years old when his father died. Nonetheless, he became an intellectual and a minister, earning a Master of Arts degree in 1604 from St. John's College in Cambridge, England. Remarkably, he was nineteen years old when he graduated and began his ministry. In 1611, he left his ministry in the northern part of England, sailed to America, and became one of the earliest settlers in Jamestown, Virginia. The following year, along with Sir Thomas Dale, he left Jamestown and traveled north along the James River with a throng of trailblazers numbering 350 in all. The group had their sights set on founding a new community, which they named Henrico. It was during that same year that Rev. Whitaker played a role in converting the Indian princess Pocahontas to Christianity after she had been taken prisoner. Adopting Rebecca as her Christian name, she was married to John Rolfe in April 1613 or 1614 at a marriage ceremony performed by Rev. Whitaker. The couple maintained their membership in Rev. Whitaker's church until they left Virginia (I am a direct descendant of Rev. Alexander Whitaker's brother, Jabez Whitaker) (Holland, Palazzolo, and Kanat).

Jordan John Whitaker, who was born in North Carolina on December 22, 1778, moved with his family to Wilkes County, Georgia, sometime before 1786. After 1794, the family then moved to Washington County, Georgia. Jordan John married Catherine, who was from South Carolina, and they moved to the Orange Hill area of Washington County, Florida, near Chipley, Florida, and eventually had three sons. William T. and James Denard survived to adulthood. James Denard Whitaker was my mother's great-grandfather, and he is a well-known figure in American history (Everett and Best; [Mrs.] J. H. Godwin, "History and Friendly Stories of Holmes County and It's [sic] Friendly People," *Holmes County [FL] Advertiser*, August 1, 1947, 2; Holland, Palazzolo, and Kanat).

James Denard Whitaker, born on October 13, 1822, in Orange Hill, Florida, is said to be the first child born in Florida after the state became a possession of the United States. Although not an incorporated community, Whitaker, Alabama, located a few miles from Slocomb, was named after him. This is the area in which James initially settled. The Whitaker Methodist Church, built in 1883, is located there. It was James who provided the lumber, land, and money to build the church. James was a towering figure of over six feet tall and was a great landowner (Everett and Best; Godwin; Holland, Palazzolo, and Kanat).

James's mother, Catherine, had two slaves, Nan and her son Pamp. In 1835, shortly after the death of James's father, Jordan John Whitaker, when James was twelve years old, he and his mother and their two slaves moved to and homesteaded an area in Geneva County, Alabama. At the time of the move, the area was located in Jackson County, Florida. Later, several boundary line shifts would occur. When Holmes County was formed, the farm became part of Holmes County, Florida. In 1853, the federal government reestablished the Florida-Alabama line, and the farm became part of Dale County, Alabama. A few years later, Alabama readjusted the southern boundary line of Dale County to form Geneva County. James once again found himself living in a different county. My mother used to say that beginning at age twelve her great-grandfather lived in four different counties and in two different states but drew water from the same well the whole time (Everett and Best; Godwin; Holland, Palazzolo, and Kanat).

James and his mother were sharecroppers at first with his uncle, with whom he shared profits from the sheep and cattle they raised. Pamp, who was small but strong, cleared the land along with James for the planting of crops. James and his mother sold crops the first year along with some sheep and cattle and had enough money to buy additional land from the U.S. government at $1.25 per acre. The deed was signed by Andrew Jackson himself, seventh president of the United States (Everett and Best; Godwin; Holland, Palazzolo, and Kanat).

In addition to farming and grazing cattle and sheep, James and Catherine opened up a stagecoach stop at the top of a high hill. They were known as hospitable hosts. James was also a very successful sheepherder who made a lot of money on the wool from his herds of sheep (Everett and Best; Godwin; Holland, Palazzolo, and Kanat).

Eventually James married Mary Ann Davis in Orange Hill, Washington County, Florida, and the couple had a total of seven children—five girls and two boys. James fought in the Confederate Army during the Civil War (Everett and Best; Godwin; Holland, Palazzolo, and Kanat).

One of James and Mary Ann's sons was Joseph H. Whitaker. He married Lugenia V. (Smith) Whitaker, Dr. Smith's aunt. They were my mother's grandparents. The family had five children, including my mother's mom, Ada Myrli (Whitaker) Armstrong, and my mother's three aunts, Luta Mae, Alice Dixie ("Dixie"), and Mary Lee (Whitaker) Rice. They also had a son, Joseph A. Whitaker, who died as an infant. Joseph raised cattle and was a bootlegger. Each year, he drove his cattle to market in Chipley, Washington County, Florida. While in Chipley, he picked up the liquor that he would later sell when he returned home. But he had a good heart. He used some of his wealth to lend money to a group

9

of doctors to help fund the building of Chipley's first hospital (Everett and Best; Godwin; Holland, Palazzolo, and Kanat).

The other prominent family in Geneva County during those days was the Smith family, related to the Whitakers through Lugenia Smith Whitaker and intermarriage. (Lugenia was the sister of George Washington Smith, Dr. Smith's father.)

At one time, in the early 1800s, in the area between Slocomb and Fadette (a small community located south of Slocomb), in a radius of less than five miles, there were five George Smiths. One of them was George Washington Smith, a Civil War veteran, and he was the father of Dr. Gordon Wright Smith. George Washington Smith was born August 31, 1839, in Alabama.

George Washington Smith's father was Daniel Ulysses Smith, born February 10, 1820, in Georgia. He married Nancy Hinson and they had eleven children. Upon their deaths, Daniel and Nancy were buried in New Hope Primitive Baptist Church Cemetery in Taylor, Houston County, Alabama.

According to the 1880 U.S. Cen-

Grave site of Daniel Ulysses Smith
(grandfather of Gordon Wright Smith).

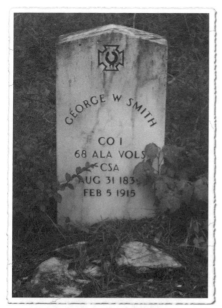

Grave site of George W. Smith
(father of Gordon Wright Smith).

sus, George, age forty-one at the time, and Rebecca, age thirty-four at the time, had six children: daughter Emily Sarah, age seventeen; daughter Nancy J., age fifteen; daughter Mary F., age thirteen; daughter Georgia Ann, age eleven; son Gordon Wright, age nine; and son Columbus Washington, age five months. Son Arthur S. Smith would come along later. The family was living in East Half Geneva, Geneva County, at the time. Following Rebecca's death in February 1894, George W. remarried.

At age sixty, according to the 1900 U.S. Census, George W. was married to Sarah A., age fifty, and living in Wrights

Creek, Geneva County. At that time, the couple's son, Arthur, age thirteen, and a housekeeper/cook, Elizabeth Pope, age fifty-five, were living with them. George Washington Smith died on February 5, 1915. Upon his death, he was buried in Smith Cemetery in Dothan, Alabama, along with his first wife, Rebecca (genealogist Tillie Van Sickle).

Daniel Ulysses Smith probably had no idea that his grandson would one day be among those doctors whose framed photographs smiled down from the wall above the soda fountain in Dalton's Drug Store. Gordon Wright Smith, one of the sons of George Washington Smith and Rebecca A. (McAllister) Smith, was born in Geneva County on October 14, 1871, and was raised on his father's farm and attended public school.

Gordon Wright Smith came from a political family, a family of strong Republicans—unusual for the predominantly Democratic area of Geneva County at the time. He was well respected. After all, he was a medical doctor. He was a formidable presence in a small town of mostly uneducated people. He had gone to college and to medical school. He graduated in June 1889 from the Abbeville branch of the Alabama Polytechnic Institute and went on to study medicine for two years at the Louisville Medical College. He served an internship at the Louisville (Kentucky) City Hospital from 1891 to 1892, during which time he also was inspector of the Jefferson Penitentiary at Jefferson, Indiana. For two years, beginning in 1892, he practiced medicine at Sanders Cross Roads in Geneva County and then at Fadette in Geneva County until 1905 (Harris Holmes).

Dr. Gordon Wright Smith.

After that Dr. Smith moved to Slocomb, where for many years his practice covered a wide section of the county. He purportedly "gained special attention for his skill in the diseases of women and children and as a skilled surgeon." For years he was the oldest physician and surgeon in Geneva County. Dr. Smith did postgraduate work at the Jefferson Medical College at Philadelphia, specializing in diseases of women and children. He also did postgraduate work on diseases of women at the Johns Hopkins University in Baltimore in 1910. In addition, in 1912, he took a special course in surgery at the New York Polyclinic (*The Heritage of Geneva County, Alabama*, Geneva, AL).

Dr. Gordon Wright Smith was well respected around Slocomb in the early 1920s. He, like the other four doctors in the city, had his faithful and loyal patients for whom he cared. He delivered babies and cared for them while also tending to their mothers and fathers. In 1920, according to the U.S. Census, Dr. Smith and his family were living on White Street in Slocomb, and Dr. Smith was forty-eight.

Dr. Gordon Wright Smith's mansion in Slocomb, Alabama.

Aunt Dixie, his second wife and my great-aunt, was thirty-seven, and two of his sons by his first wife, Gordon Royce (age twenty-three) and Atkinson Angus (age nineteen), were living with them along with Moody Tew, Aunt Dixie's son by her first marriage. Clyde, Dr. Smith's oldest son by his first wife, Theodora, was married and was living with his family.

Dr. Smith served several terms as County Health Officer and as Slocomb's City Health Officer. He volunteered for service during World War I and served as a member of the Medical Reserve Corps. He was on duty during the influenza epidemic in northern Alabama. He served several terms as president of the Geneva County Medical Society and was a member of the Alabama State Medical Society, as well as a member of the American Medical Association. For a number of years he was local surgeon for the Central of Georgia Railway Company and for the Morris Lumber Company of Slocomb during a time when it was common practice for large companies to have their own surgeons on staff or to have designated surgeons assigned to them (*The Heritage of Geneva County, Alabama,* Geneva, AL).

It is very likely that Dr. Smith was held in high regard. We know that he had money. It could be assumed that he had a lot of power. He served on boards. He owned many businesses. He was sole proprietor of the Smith Telephone Company in Slocomb. He was a director of the Smith Hardwood Lumber Company at Slocomb and for a number of years served as its local surgeon. He was a member of the Board of Stewards of the Methodist Episcopal Church, South; past senior warden of Lodge No. 599, F.&A.M.; member of Dothan Chapter No. 113, Royal Arch Masons; Dothan Commandery No. 25, Knights Templar; chancellor of Slocomb Lodge No. 232, Knights of Pythias; a delegate to the Grand Lodge of the Knights of Pythias; and a consul of Slocomb Camp No. 310, Woodmen of the World. He also was a member of Slocomb Camp, Modern Woodmen of America, the Modern Order of Praetorians, and Dothan Lodge, B.P.O. Elks (Harris Holmes).

Dr. Smith owned a lot of land, including the Dean Mill, a water-powered grist and seed mill two miles northwest of Slocomb, where he maintained a large fish pond, which was kept stocked with black bass and bluegill courtesy of the government. In Geneva County alone, he had hundreds of acres of farming land, as well as property in Slocomb, including his home. Between January 1890 and October 1929, Dr. Smith registered deeds for at least eighteen parcels of land in Geneva County alone, totaling at least 1,810 acres and at a cost of at least $4,760—a lot of acres and a lot of money back then (Geneva County Records).

Recognizing the darker side of the times, Dr. Smith probably had his hand in sharecropping, one of the most exploitive industries the nation has ever known. The faces of the South showed the effects of years of poverty: faces drawn by worry, work, and wear; depleted, blighted faces. Perhaps no faces showed this more than those of the thousands forced into the system of sharecropping. Sharecroppers were those who were tenants on the land of a landowner who allowed the tenants to work the land in return for a share of the crop produced, for example, 50 percent.

McDaniel, Georgia,
from *You Have Seen Their Faces*.

After the Civil War and the devastation that it had wrought on the South, landowners had little money to pay out for wages or taxes. Likewise, former slaves had labor to offer, but in general no land. The sharecropping system made sense because there was such an abundance of cotton, and it could generate a lot of income for landowners, croppers, merchants, and tax collectors. In Geneva County, cotton growing began when the lumber business died out in 1911. In 1929, there were as many black as white sharecroppers in Geneva County. They had a presence in the entire area, and they lived in what were known as shanty houses. In 1933, when President Franklin Delano Roosevelt took office and after the banks closed during the 1933 banking crisis, many—

13

whites and blacks alike—were left homeless and were forced into sharecropping.

To demonstrate just how devastating the system of sharecropping was, it even brought black and white workers together in the South in 1934. In the summer of that year, a remarkable historical event took place when black and white sharecroppers and tenant farmers in eastern Arkansas banded together to form a protest movement against the sharecropping system. The Southern Tenant Farmers Union (STFU) was formed in an effort to try to gain some economic security following the collapse of the plantation system. By 1936, the organization consisted of more than 25,000 members in Arkansas, Missouri, Oklahoma, Tennessee, and Texas, and it had become recognized nationally under the New Deal as a mechanism for speaking and lobbying on behalf of the rights of sharecroppers. However, its efforts were thwarted by many external and internal pressures (Trudier Harris, "Sharecropping," http://www.english.illinois.edu/maps/poets/a_f/brown/sharecropping.htm).

Dr. Smith probably used his hundreds of acres of land for sharecropping. If so, he may have exploited the poor—both white and black alike. The land remained in his family for generations and may have been sharecropped. The land extended to the southern portion of Geneva County to the Florida line and perhaps into Florida. Later, some of his descendants used the land to harvest pine trees to generate income. Clyde was very much into growing pine trees, and he, too, may have continued with the sharecropping. Some of the land that Clyde Smith inherited is probably still in the Smith family.

Happy Hollow, Georgia, from *You Have Seen Their Faces.*

Not much is known about Clyde's two brothers, Gordon Royce, a medical doctor, and Atkinson Angus, an attorney, except for the fact that Gordon Royce's draft card lists him as medium build with brown eyes and dark hair, and Clyde Smith's draft card shows him as short and stout with blue eyes and black hair. We do know that today, Stephen Smith (born 1950), a direct descendant of Benjamin Franklin Smith, the brother of Dr. Smith's father, serves as a Circuit Court judge in Geneva County, Alabama, having been elected in November 2010 (Van Sickle).

Some say that the South has always been and will always be old, meaning that hardship, poverty, and exploitation and their devastating effects are inherent and will live on in this part of the nation. What is for certain is that the life of the sharecropper, only a step away from that of the slave, was one of misery. Some refer to it as a new form of slavery. Even though the system provided tenants with access to land, they were still tied to the land and heavily supervised by the landowner. For blacks, it was a system that was often impossible at which to win or in which to keep afloat. Blacks often were responsible for purchasing all the equipment, seed, and fertilizer they needed for their "business," and the only way they could do this was to borrow from the local bank and purchase their groceries and supplies from the local general store on credit. By the end of the season, they often did not have enough money to pay off the bank and the merchant, so they began the new year with a deficit. Their lives were somewhat equivalent to today's consumer who finds it impossible to escape his credit card debt, which continues to rise. Blacks' only recourse often was to flee in the night and run away to the North, the utopia of freedom and opportunity (Harris).

While impoverished blacks certainly were exploited under the sharecropping system, poor whites had it about as bad. Children in tattered clothes, with no shoes or socks, were kept home from school to work the land along with their parents, and they knew nothing but the emptiness and backbreaking drudgery of tilling the parched, sandy, or clay-like soil for what meager returns the land would provide. Women with hands like shoe leather, brittle hair and skin, and dirt embedded deep beneath their fingernails

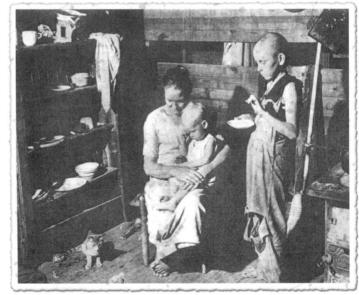

Peterson, Alabama, from *You Have Seen Their Faces.*

15

worked the cotton lands—women with rotten teeth and handmade burlap bonnets to help mitigate the harsh effects of the hot, blazing sun. Torn pages from magazines made the covering for the shanties' walls—a makeshift wallpaper. One single bed might serve an entire family. But they were never too tired or their knees too sore to kneel down and thank God for what He had provided.

We can only imagine the influence Dr. Smith had, and how he used that influence on people. While we do not know and may never know for sure, speculation might lead one to assume that perhaps he used that influence especially on women, the weak, and the most vulnerable, both black and white.

# Chapter 3

## Getting Away with Murder:
### The Murders of Theodora "Dera" Atkinson, James Isaac Tew, Alice Dixie (Whitaker) Smith ("Aunt Dixie"), and James Moody Tew

It is said that life is not fair. Nothing could have been closer to the truth back in Slocomb and Geneva County in the 1920s.

In a November 16, 1928, *Geneva County (AL) Reaper* newspaper article, the journalist writes about the sorry state of things in Slocomb, Alabama, and the apparent inequities in the legal system. He writes that a black man recently was sentenced to the state farm for twenty-five years for stealing a small amount of property. He bemoans the fact that human life apparently has become a cheap commodity, citing the example of a white man a few weeks prior who had shot a neighbor over a trivial dispute and received a sentence of only five years. The writer expresses disbelief at how two months had passed following the brutal murder of Slocomb High School principal Claud F. Avant, and yet the murderer, or murderers, had not yet been apprehended. He chastises the system for its lackadaisical handling of the case, writing that there has not been an obvious effort made by law enforcement officials to locate the perpetrators of the crime and expressing the opinion that murder is apparently a safe crime ("Murder a Safe Crime," *Geneva County [AL] Reaper*, November 16, 1928).

"I just want to say that it ain't right to kill me for something I didnt' [*sic*] do." That was a quote by a black man upon being escorted out of an Alabama courtroom and off to Kilby Prison in 1928 for the crime of assaulting a white woman. It took the jury only two and a half hours of deliberation to find nineteen-year-old Mose Daniels guilty of criminally attacking a young Montgomery white woman and to decide that he should die in the electric chair for the crime, thus substantiating the contention in the above-referenced article that human life seemed to have lost all value ("Murder a Safe Crime"; "To Die in Electric Chair for Assault on Woman," unidentified newspaper clipping, 1928).

Wealthy, high-profile white men could work the system to their advantage in the 1920s in the South. The man able to employ high-priced attorneys could get away with virtually anything, as many would argue is still the case today in many parts of the country and the world. Women and blacks were most often victims of prejudicial, biased, and discriminating judicial and social systems. A front-page article from the May 27, 1930, *Dothan (AL) Eagle* reports that a seventy-year-old woman was sentenced to a year at the state farm for women in Little Rock, Arkansas, after being convicted on charges of violating the liquor laws. Mary Smith appealed the sentence, but her appeal was denied and the senior citizen was carted off to the pen by order of the Supreme Court ("Woman Goes to Pen," *Dothan [AL] Eagle*, May 27, 1930, 1).

A few weeks later, on June 13, 1930, a black Montgomery, Alabama, automobile mechanic was sentenced to fifteen years in the state penitentiary for armed robbery. After J. H. Keith took sixty-five dollars from the cash register of a filling station at gunpoint, a Montgomery Circuit Court jury took only about four hours to render its verdict in the case ("J. H. Keith Gets 15 Years for Filling Station Robbery," *Geneva County [AL] Reaper*, June 13, 1930, 1).

Blacks in the South were denigrated in the press and made to appear dangerous—a force to be feared. One newspaper account describes the case of twenty-eight-year-old Frank McCoy, a black man and former convict (whose record undoubtedly did not help his case) who was put away in Kilby Prison for "safekeeping" (presumably for a long term) on a charge of allegedly attacking a white woman. The alleged assault was said to have occurred while the man was serving a term for robbery in Jefferson County, Alabama ("Negro in Kilby for Safe Keeping Today," *Dothan [AL] Eagle*, December 18, 1929, 1).

Partiality and inequity were rampant throughout these years in the South. Men of prominence and stature—white men who had the means and connections— could easily get away with illegal and immoral activity, including murder. At one point in my childhood, Enterprise, Alabama, had a shootout/knife fight right in the middle of the downtown section involving the deputy sheriff and the chief of police, in which Deputy Sheriff Walker Thomas was gunned down and his murderer, Chief of Police J. M. Whigham, walked away from the crime. My mom told me the story herself. It took place back in early June 1940, while Mom, my brother T. E., and I were living in Enterprise, Coffee County, Alabama. Coffee County adjoins Geneva County, and Enterprise is only about twenty-five miles from the city of Slocomb.

Would someone in Dr. Smith's capacity or of Dr. Smith's stature ever have been sent to the state pen for violating the liquor laws? Would the Supreme Court have convicted him had he been found guilty of hiding a bottle of booze in between the mattresses of his bed or under the seat of his car? Perhaps it's foolish to think that a warrant would ever have been issued to search his premises or property. Perhaps if such a charge were to be brought against him, he might say that the liquor was for medicinal purposes. What if someone of Dr. Smith's stature had stolen money or property? Would he even have been charged for such a crime? Perhaps the case would not have escalated to the judicial system. And what about assault? Someone in his position might be able to turn any charge around to make it appear that he was the victim.

I will let the reader decide; however, many believed that by virtue of his money and his influence, Dr. Gordon W. Smith and his accomplices got away with murder and that he literally got away—staging his own death and fleeing Slocomb, although for years he had given every appearance of being an upstanding physician and model citizen. His marriages seemed normal on the surface, but they were far from that. To some, Dr. Smith, it seems, would have done anything to get what he wanted, including the woman he desired—and anything included murder.

On July 9, 1893, at the age of twenty-two, Dr. Smith married Theodora Atkinson. They had three sons: Cornelius Clyde (known as Clyde), Dr. Gordon Royce, and Atkinson Angus, an attorney. Theodora died in January 1918, and in July 1919, Dr. Smith married Alice Dixie (Whitaker) Smith, my mother's aunt.

Aunt Dixie was born on November 9, 1882, in Geneva County, Alabama. Her mother, Lugenia (Smith) Whitaker, as indicated, was Dr. Smith's aunt. She had four siblings: Aunt Luta, who also married a Smith, James M. Smith, a direct descendant of Dr. Smith's family; my grandmother, Ada Myrli (Whitaker) Armstrong; Aunt Mary Lee (Whitaker) Rice; and a brother, Joseph A.

Lugenia V. (Smith) Whitaker (seated on the right).
One of her four daughters,
Mary Lee (Whitaker) Rice, is seated on the left.
Mary's daughter, Montez (Rice) Grantham,
and granddaughter, are standing.

19

Whitaker, who died young.

Aunt Luta and her husband, James, ended up with the Whitaker fortune upon the death of Lugenia, her mother, on March 6, 1922, since all of her siblings and her father, Joseph H. Whitaker, had predeceased her mother. (Joseph H. Whitaker, Lugenia's husband, predeceased her on January 27, 1917.) Aunt Luta died in 1948 and her husband, James Smith, died in 1962. Thus, you could say that the Whitaker wealth was controlled by a Smith for forty years.

After James's death, their only child, Letha, born December 3, 1907, who died on January 14, 2000, was left everything. Thus, she controlled the Whitaker wealth for another thirty-eight years.

Aunt Dixie's marriage to Dr. Smith in July 1919, at about age thirty-seven, was a second marriage for her as well. According to the 1910 U.S. Census, Dr. Smith had two servants, Leola and Will Hall. It is not known how Aunt Dixie and Dr. Smith met, but it is safe to assume that, in a small community, with them being second cousins, they would have had the opportunity to socialize with one another on more than one occasion, and probably on a regular basis. Life was close-knit in Geneva County, especially for relatives. We also know that, like her sister and my grandmother, Ada Myrli (Armstrong) Whitaker, Aunt Dixie was a beautiful woman, and it isn't too far-fetched to say that Dr. Smith would have been interested in her.

Aunt Dixie had married James Isaac Tew in about 1897. He was born in 1877 in Barbour County, Alabama, the son of John William Tew and Minerva Dykes. According to the 1900 U.S. Census, James Isaac, twenty-three years of age, was a farmer living in Wrights Creek, Geneva County, and was married to Aunt Dixie, age twenty-three.

According to the 1910 U.S. Census, James Isaac owned a farm free and clear but lived in a home in town and worked as a merchant in a dry goods store. Aunt Dixie worked as a saleswoman in a department store (probably in a separate business). James Isaac and Aunt Dixie had two children: Dixie Valeria Tew, born February 1, 1898, in Fadette, Alabama, and James Moody Tew, born January 8, 1915, in Geneva County, Alabama. (Dixie Valeria had a son who later became mayor of Slocomb and another son who became an attorney.)

At the time of Aunt Dixie's marriage to Dr. Smith, her son Moody Tew was

Grave site of James Isaac Tew,
Aunt Dixie's first husband, who was allegedly
murdered by Dr. Gordon Wright Smith.

living with them. Also living with Aunt Dixie and Dr. Smith were his three sons from his marriage to Theodora Atkinson. Aunt Dixie and Dr. Smith lived in a huge, beautiful colonial house in Slocomb at the corner of Morris Street and White Street (Alabama Highway 52). Claud F. Avant, the principal of Slocomb High School, was boarding with them. Everyone referred to him as Professor Avant. According to my mother, Professor Avant and Dixie became good friends. Also according to my mother, the root of Dr. Smith and Aunt Dixie's problems was that both had been married before and the fact that they had Professor Avant boarding with them (Holland, Palazzolo, and Kanat).

Through my mother's interview, it was revealed that Aunt Dixie knew that Dr. Smith had murdered his first wife, Theodora Atkinson. My mother also revealed that Aunt Dixie knew that Dr. Smith had murdered Aunt Dixie's first husband, James Isaac Tew, so that he could marry her. James Isaac had died in 1915 at age thirty-eight—one of Dr. Smith's unsuspecting victims, and one of the crimes for which he was never charged. Presumably Dr. Smith murdered Theodora Atkinson so that he could marry Aunt Dixie.

But Aunt Dixie certainly would never have suspected when she married Dr. Smith that he would harm her. I'm sure she felt safe and secure at first. Whether he truly loved her or whether he had enticed and charmed her into believing he loved her and would care for her for the rest of her life is uncertain and will never be known. But I'm sure that the prestige of being married to one of the most powerful and wealthiest men in Slocomb and in Geneva County was an allure, and Aunt Dixie must have felt like a queen in his presence. Their lifestyle exceeded that which she had had with Isaac Tew, a farmer and store employee and possibly owner, and equaled that which she had known as a child of Joseph H. and Lugenia V. (Smith) Whitaker, one of the most prominent and wealthiest families in the county. She undoubtedly felt well taken care of and protected—by his wealth, influence, and power. Perhaps, too, Aunt Dixie felt controlled by Dr. Smith out of fear.

It is appropriate to note here that although the Joseph H. Whitaker family enjoyed extreme wealth, there were exceptions. One that is particularly noteworthy is the case of

Grave site of Walter Eugene Armstrong (my grandfather).

21

Ada Myrli (Whitaker) Armstrong, Joseph Whitaker's daughter and my grand-mother, whose husband was Walter Eugene Armstrong. Walter sold the eighty-one acres of land that his father, John Ludwell Armstrong, and the forty acres that Joseph H. Whitaker had given him and squandered the proceeds, becoming a sharecropper and day laborer. (Joseph and Lugenia Whitaker disowned this daughter and her children and refused to assist them in need, and this was the principal reason why they even refused to attend this daughter's funeral.)

When my mother was only six years old, her mother died, and her father, Wal-

Walter Eugene and Ada Myrli (Whitaker) Armstrong
(my grandfather and grandmother).

ter Eugene, who could not support his youngest six children, divided them up at his wife's grave site, turning their custody over to his brothers, sister, and their spouses. My mother went to live with her Uncle John and Aunt Ophelia, who originally were reluctant to take her.

Uncle John did not like Walter Eugene and was extremely angry with him. Walter Eugene had said that he couldn't care for his younger children, but after the funeral he went to Miami, Florida, to live for a while. My mother heard from someone that while he was there, he had tried out for the Florida Marlins, a minor league baseball team, despite being about forty years of age. When he was much younger, he had played in the Alabama League. Walter remarried soon after Ada Myrli's death and started having another large family. He couldn't support that family either.

Shortly after returning from Miami, he married a woman named Idella Tate, a humongous sixteen-year-old girl, only nine years older than my mother. He began having children with her immediately. It was into that environment that my mother next found herself immersed, with two baby half-sisters, Margie and Annie Pearl, for whom she cared.

My mother, a descendant of the wealthy Whitakers, would live this way—being bounced from one house to another—for the better part of her young life. After she married and had my brother and me, she ended up divorced only a few years later, a single woman left to raise two young boys on her own. She worked

Mertice Mae (Armstrong) Holland: 1916-1990.

the rest of her life in minimum-wage jobs in order to raise us, doing everything from spinning cotton into thread at a mill to waitressing to cleaning cylinders in a plant built for developing nuclear material for use in the atomic bomb. Life for her and for us was never easy, and some would say it is a miracle that we made it.

Getting back to the story of Aunt Dixie, she soon began to feel ill. One day, as she was lying sick in bed, as the story goes, Professor Avant came into the house at noon and walked down the hall to her room. When he approached the bedroom door and asked her how she was doing, she responded, "Well, I guess I'm feeling all right, but I think I will go just like Dr. Smith's first wife and my first husband." This is directly from my mother's interview tape. My mother said that her father, Walter Eugene Armstrong, is the one who told her that Dr. Smith was the one who was thought to have given Aunt Dixie's first husband something to kill him and that Dr. Smith had also done away with his first wife (Holland, Palazzolo, and Kanat).

My mother said that at first what Aunt Dixie had told Professor Avant had thrown him into shock. But then he made the mistake of trying to take advantage of the situation. He knew that Aunt Dixie was suggesting that Dr. Smith had killed his first wife and her first husband with poison. Professor Avant tried to blackmail Dr. Smith for three thousand dollars, according to my mother. (Some accounts indicate this amount was three hundred dollars.) She described Dr. Smith as a "shrewd old cookie" (Mertice Mae Armstrong, interview by Eudon Holland, December 26, 1987).

Aunt Dixie just kept getting sicker and sicker. My mother said that if she had to guess, she would say that Aunt Dixie died of poisoning.

After Aunt Dixie's death on January 23, 1928, Moody went to live with a first cousin, Charlie Embanks, in Slocomb. It appears as though Moody moved out of Dr. Smith's house after Aunt Dixie's death when he was thirteen years old, possibly indicating that he was afraid of Dr. Smith.

As previously stated, Dr. Smith had gained special attention for his skill in the diseases of women and children. Can it be assumed that he would know the weaknesses and vulnerabilities of women and children? Can it be assumed

Grave site of Alice Dixie Whitaker Smith (Aunt Dixie), wife of Dr. Gordon Wright Smith.

that he would be able to readily get his hands on any kind of poison he wanted at any time? It is said that death by poison is difficult to detect, even today, unless one knows what to look for. After all, Dr. Smith was a "shrewd old cookie," according to my mother. Can it be deduced that someone with Dr. Smith's medical background and his knowledge, skill, and expertise would know just how to go about poisoning someone and that he would know how to keep it from being detected (Harris Holmes; Mertice Mae Armstrong interview)?

Dr. Smith remarried after Aunt Dixie's death and fathered a son, George W., with his third wife, Gussie. Gussie was born in Florida in 1896 and was a nurse by profession (Van Sickle). It is interesting to note that Gussie was also a McAllister and that she and Dr. Smith were related. They were distant cousins. Meanwhile, Dr. Smith supposedly died of heart failure on January 26, 1930, before Lee Phillips was to be tried for Avant's murder on June 9, 1930. But there was more than speculation surrounding his death and whether he actually died or whether in reality he staged his own death and fled the scene.

Aunt Dixie's son, Moody, died unexpectedly, too. My mother vividly remembered hearing about his death from her grandmother Lugenia (Smith) Whitaker. He was only seventeen years old and a freshman at Auburn University in Alabama, living in a boarding house. My mother remembered hearing her grandmother tell her that she had packed Moody's trunk before he went to enroll in school. Then suddenly, on the morning of Friday, March 4, 1932, Moody woke up and told the housemother what he wanted for breakfast: a fried egg and a little hoecake. He walked into the bathroom to get ready for class and supposedly had a heart attack and died.

My mother said that she never did understand how someone so young could just die like that. She

Grave site of Dr. Gordon Wright Smith.

would always feel bad for him when she heard that story. She always felt someone so young did not deserve to die, especially someone whose stepfather had been charged with murder and whose mother was possibly killed by his stepfather.

Mysteriously, Moody's death certificate lists "acute alcoholism" as the cause of death. His body was found on Saturday, March 5. The informant, Moody's guardian, A. A. Smith, of Hartford, Alabama, accompanied the body to the Houston Funeral Home in Dothan, where, interestingly, the funeral took place on Sunday, March 6, only one day after the body was found. Moody, a seventeen-year-old business administration student, died while at college, and his body was immediately removed to the funeral home. It's curious that this young student would not have been laid out for at least a couple of days so that his friends and family could pay their respects. Certainly money wasn't an issue. After all, he was the stepson of the late Dr. Gordon W. Smith and the grandson of Joseph Whitaker, two of the wealthiest men in Geneva County. However, of great significance is the fact that it is believed that Dr. Smith carried a lot of insurance on Moody Tew, as well as on Aunt Dixie.

Also interesting is that the college surgeon, Dr. B. F. Thomas, reported to the press that "acute indigestion" was the cause of death. Did Dr. Smith have some influence on what was reported by this college surgeon, if he, himself, had not actually died and was still around to have a say in what was reported to the public about Moody's death? After all, the medical community was a small circle back then, especially in the South and in such communities as Dothan, Geneva County, and Auburn. Either way, neither "acute alcoholism" nor "acute indigestion" seems like a plausible cause of death for a seventeen-year-old.

And it's very unusual that his death seems to have been wrapped up so quickly and tidily. After all, in those days, it was customary for a body to be laid out for at least four to five days to accommodate the travel needs of family and friends. It often took days for people to travel from one place to another, in a time when most people in that area did not own automobiles and traveled primarily by mule-drawn wagon. And Dr. Smith's insurance policy on Moody would have reverted to his new wife upon his death, so she would have been the beneficiary under the policy ("Auburn Freshman Discovered Dead Early This A.M.," *The Plainsman [Auburn, AL]*, March 5, 1932) (provided by Rev. Cliff Knight, a direct Whitaker descendant).

Nobody ever figured out what the official cause of death was of both Aunt Dixie and Moody Tew. My mother said it will remain one of those mysteries that's buried deep in the South.

Claud F. Avant (artist's rendering).

# Chapter 4

## Not Killed Where Found:
### The Murder of Professor Claud F. Avant

There is an expression that good people die at an early age. It may even be a proverb. Popular songwriter and recording artist Billy Joel even wrote a song about it ("Only the Good Die Young"). And in many cases, the saying applies. The case of Slocomb High School Principal Claud F. Avant is one of them.

Claud Fitzgerald Avant was born on May 15, 1890, in Equality, Alabama, a small community in Coosa County, Alabama, which derives its name from the Creek Indian tribe. His father was John G. Avant and his mother was Julia Augusta Mathews. Claud was the third of nine children. As a young man, he started out in farming before he went into teaching. He was a tall, attractive, athletically built, blue-eyed, blond-haired man. He soon became the beloved principal of Slocomb High School—the fifth to serve in that position.

The first principal of Slocomb High School was N. B. (Bud) Hughes. Subsequent principals were Jim Marley, G. C. Moseley, H. T. Wallace, and then Claud. In 1925, the two-story school, built by James Joshua Kelley, grandfather of Max and Tony Kelly, who helped provide research for this story, burned down (the spelling of Kelley was changed in the family line). After the fire, a new structure was built. Claud was instrumental in "the standardization and unprecedented growth of the new school" (Harris Holmes). Later, in 1928, a new brick elementary school building was added. Slocomb, it seems, was booming.

During the 1928–29 school year, Slocomb High School's teachers were J. D. Gibson (Coach), Annie L. Carroll, Elizabeth Hightower, Niva Mae Olive, Willie Marley, Athena Church, Lula Mae Newton, Melba Sellers, Celeste Foster, Clara Goare, Irene Woodham, S. D. Lowe, Eleanor Clark, and Willie Jim Faircloth. As the king and queen and their attendants emerged from beneath blue and white arches and marched proudly in the annual May Day Festival of 1928, thirty-seven-year-old Claud F. Avant was at the forefront of it all, leading the queen, Flora Foster (later Dalton), with her bouquet of white American Beauty roses embellished with a cascade of green fern. Her king was Adolph Justice, and their attendants were Mozell Norrell, Ann Northington, Elosie Baker, Lola Underwood, Bernice Martin (later Hornsby), and Myrl Davis (later Smith). The page was M. V. Holley. Each class presented the queen with a bouquet of flowers. It would seem to be a snapshot out of picture-perfect small-town America. But all was not to remain perfect for long in Slocomb (Harris Holmes).

Soon thereafter, on September 23, 1928, news erupted to the shock and dismay of all of Slocomb that six-foot-two, one-hundred-ninety-six-pound Claud Avant, adored by all of Slocomb, had suddenly and mysteriously disappeared after having served four years as principal of Slocomb High (Harris Holmes).

All of Slocomb skidded to a halt. The town was stunned. Students were overcome with sorrow. Teachers and citizens were beside themselves. Slocomb's chief of police, J. C. Hallford, scurried to organize a search crew. Even one of Professor Avant's brothers joined in the search. Grief-stricken, the whole town anxiously awaited news from the authorities.

Claud's father and brothers came forward stating that they knew of no one who would want to harm him. All evidence revealed that the principal's life had been an open book and that there were no secrets looming in his life. Suicide was considered, but all who knew Professor Avant attested to the fact that he had loved life, so that theory was ruled out. Robbery was not a motive since it was determined that Professor Avant had neither taken any money out of the bank nor withdrawn anything from his safety deposit box prior to his disappearance.

An excerpt from "The Knife" by Dr. D. D. Stephens reads as follows:

> *Thus, on Tuesday morning two days after he had vanished, groups of men stood on street corners, discussing the mystery, while automobiles whizzed into town from the adjacent countryside, filled with others equally concerned, for the news had traveled fast and far. A crowd gathered in Slocomb's main business section, where a stout man with drooping mustache and small eyes that squinted behind shell-rimmed glasses sought to address it. The man was Dr. G.W. Smith, at whose home the missing school principal boarded. A hush fell upon the crowd, as the physician, his voice filled with emotion, began to speak. "My friends," he said, then paused. His emotions [sic] was plainly too much for him. The words choked in his throat. At this point, a cousin of the speaker, standing next to him, touched the physician lightly on the arm. "Speak up, Doctor," he said calmly, "so all can hear you."*
> *Regaining his composure somewhat, Dr. Smith continued. "My friends," he said huskily, "Professor Avant, as you all know, has mysteriously disap-*

*peared. He was last seen with us Sunday afternoon when he was seen driving his car north out of Slocomb. Where or why he has gone none of us know. It may be he had trouble of some sort, for he recently told my wife he had received a letter that worried him so he could neither eat nor sleep, and this may be the cause of his disappearance. Or it may be he has temporarily lost his memory and is just driving on and on."*

Dr. Smith's voice grew stronger with resolute purpose.

*"But whatever it is, let every one of us do all in our power to find him. If there has been foul play, as some of you seem to feel, let us scour the country-side. I don't think it is of any use to go south, for he was last seen going north, so let us concentrate on every swamp and slough within a radius of twenty miles to the north of us. I know them all and I can direct you to each of them. Let our watchword be Find Avant!"*

Meanwhile, the intensive investigation continued. Leads were followed up on, but nothing came of them until finally, a big break. At around noon on Friday, September 28, it was announced that the body of a man had been found in a swamp about twenty-eight miles southwest of Slocomb, near Bonifay, Florida, on the Alabama-Florida state line. The body was found by J. D. Davis, the son of a farmer in the area, who heard the sound of hogs snarling and preying on the poor man's body. He followed the angry sounds, which led him to a secluded area near a slough. There, in an area that was a ways from an unimproved country road, the horrified man discovered the body and ran to the nearest telephone to report his finding (Mayor D. D. Stephens, as told to James Cato Pattillo, "The Knife," *True Detective*).

The first to arrive were Chief Hallford and policeman Ernest Davis, who were accompanied by Grover Hughes, sheriff of Geneva County. They knew immediately that the body was that of Professor Avant and that he had been brutally murdered. Investigators found in the pockets of the dead professor his watch, two fountain pens, seventy-six cents, a bunch of keys, and a deposit ticket for fifty dollars, a deposit he had made to his account with the Slocomb Bank the day before he had disappeared (Stephens).

A short while later, J. E. Sorrels, another official, arrived to help in the investigation (Stephens).

Policeman Ernest A. Davis was a mainstay in Slocomb. He was born on February 11, 1895, in Geneva County, Alabama, and was married to Laura Peel. They had three children. He had marshaled the town of Slocomb for many years and was well respected but also feared. Everyone knew that he meant business when he went to arrest someone. They knew not to cross him. When dealing with someone who had become intoxicated, many times, if that person would let him,

Davis would carry him home rather than jailing him, thus saving him the cost of fines and penalties. Davis was firm but knew how to deal with people. He would go on to serve as Slocomb's only policeman from 1924 until 1964, when he would become chief of police, a title he would hold until 1972, when he would be promoted to public service director at age seventy-seven. He would retire from that position in his eighties (Harris Holmes).

Police Chief Hallford and Sheriff Hughes summoned Dr. L. H. Paul and Dr. Dan S. Frasier, who conducted the medical examination. It was determined that the professor had been dead for four or five days but that the cool autumn air was enough to preserve the body somewhat. Cause of death was a blow to the right side of the head and a stab wound in the heart, driven with enough force to sever the cartilage in two where the rib joined the sternum. It was described as "a powerful and savage knife thrust" (Stephens).

The professor's body was lying face up with the clothing of his upper body pulled down so as to leave bare his chest and upper arms. His gray hat, which he was seen wearing at the time of his disappearance, was nowhere to be found (Stephens).

Underneath the body was found a large, new, open pocketknife with an alligator, or sawtooth, blade. The knife contained a smaller blade as well, but it was the larger, sawtooth blade that was exposed and which the two physicians believed was the blade that had been plunged into the professor's heart. Thus they believed they had found the murder weapon (Stephens).

Also discovered was a short watch chain, which was lying near the professor's feet. Because no one present at the investigation could identify the chain as belonging to Professor Avant, it was assumed that the chain, as well as the knife, belonged to the assailants, and they were considered evidence (Stephens).

It had rained intermittently all day on Sunday when the professor had disappeared, and thus the investigators opined that tracks should be visible in the wet dirt. They searched and found tracks leading from the country road to the edge of the slough. From this they concluded that the murderer or murderers had carried the body from the road to the far edge of the slough (Stephens).

Since it was autumn and leaves had fallen and had obscured the ground, every other piece of evidence that might have been visible, the investigators concluded, was completely obliterated. But since there was no blood at the scene and because there did not appear to be any signs of a struggle, they determined that the victim had not been murdered where he was found (Stephens).

J. E. Sorrels solved the mystery of the professor's missing car. He discovered the Ford coupe about one hundred yards away from the bank of the slough. It had been pushed off the country road and over the bank of the slough and had landed at the bottom of a shallow ravine. The perpetrator or perpetrators had attempted to destroy the vehicle by setting fire to it (Stephens).

Although the professor's car had been badly burned, the interior was sufficiently intact so as to provide further evidence, including a hammer. In addition, on the ledge back of the seat the investigators found a closed pocketknife, which was later identified as having belonged to Professor Avant. The burned ashes of what had formerly been a woolen cloth or blanket were also in the car. The license tag had been torn off in what appeared to be an effort to destroy the vehicle's identification. This, however, was in vain as the tag was later found on the opposite side of the slough (Stephens).

Immediately, a coroner's inquest was held, which was presided over by Judge Carswell of Holmes County, Florida, since the location of the body caused the inquest to fall within the official jurisdiction of the State of Florida. The verdict was that Claud F. Avant had been murdered by some unknown person or persons (Stephens).

The police investigators felt that with all the evidence and clues it would not be difficult to find and apprehend the murderer or murderers. Much attention seemed to focus on the watch chain and the knife. But the hammer, it seems, was not given as much attention (Stephens).

What had the investigators completely stumped was the nearly complete absence of blood on the victim's body and at the location where he was discovered. They soon pegged it as the "bloodless murder" (Stephens).

It became the mission of Mayor D. D. Stephens, as well as the state's attorney general, Charlie C. McCall, and his team of investigators, to find out who had killed Professor Avant. The men were looking into each and every possible clue. Every piece of evidence that was uncovered, including the knife that was found underneath the professor's body, the watch chain, and the professor's clothing, which had been held by Sheriff Hughes, were all turned over to the state's investigators (Stephens).

Attorney General McCall had an excellent track record in the area of crime investigation for the State of Alabama, and he personally oversaw the Avant murder case. He took as his assistant field investigator W. J. Courtney, along with detectives H. B. Reid and H. R. Elliott, who served as the state's investigators. W. J. Purvis, the local veterinarian, worked undercover (Stephens).

One of the primary clues in the case was a short watch chain that had been found near Professor Avant's body. After some investigation among the farmers of the area, Detective Purvis discovered that Lee Phillips, a fifty-year-old Slocomb farmer residing near Smith's mill, had attempted to sell a watch chain to a Hartford man for three dollars. The description of the chain matched that of the chain owned by Professor Avant, which had been given to him as a Christmas present by his fellow teachers at Slocomb High. His watch chain had gone missing prior to when his body was found; thus, it was believed that the chain that Phillips attempted to sell may have been Professor Avant's (Stephens).

It was also discovered that a few days after Avant had disappeared, Phillips had visited his brother-in-law, Green Crutchfield, who lived in Florida, and purportedly had confessed to him. Chief of Police Hallford and the state's investigator called on Crutchfield and questioned him about Lee Phillips's visit. Crutchfield told them frankly that Phillips had paid him a visit a few days after Claud Avant's disappearance while he was fishing at Collins Mill. He said that Phillips was very nervous and told him something that "took his breath away," stating that Claud Avant's murder had been committed in the school building office in Slocomb (Stephens).

This prompted an investigation by Mayor Stephens into the school's office. He found "curious-looking specks" on six of the chairs in the office after examining all of them in his laboratory. Specks were also found on some papers and a catalog that were found on Professor Avant's desk. Mayor Stephens had the chairs, papers, and catalog tested to see if the specks were human blood, and the analysis confirmed that the specks were in fact human blood. However, they were merely specks, which baffled the investigators, who continued to be mystified by the "bloodless stabbing" (Stephens).

Meanwhile, Professor Avant's funeral was held on Saturday, September 29, almost a week from the day of his disappearance, and one day after his body was found. The services were held in the Methodist Church in Slocomb, with the Rev. D. Y. Register, the church's pastor, presiding over the burial services. It was reported that nearly the entire community turned out to pay "their last tribute of respect and affection to the memory of one whose honesty, friendliness, and usefulness had endeared him to all who knew him. Then, accompanied by sorrowing relatives and friends, the remains were carried to Equality, Alabama, where the elder Avant lived, for burial" (Stephens).

Claud F. Avant in woods.

Following the funeral, the investigation continued. What was known was that Professor Avant was last seen between Hartford and Slocomb at about four o'clock on Sunday afternoon, September 23, when he apparently left Slocomb for Hartford to visit a lady friend. Each day, the residents of Slocomb anxiously awaited and hastily snatched up their copies of the local newspapers, which were filled with numerous accounts of the events leading up to the murdered professor's disappearance. Everyone eagerly hoped to read an article stating that something had been uncovered that had led to the clue that would break the case, ensnare the killer or killers, and once again ensure Slocomb's security (Stephens). Several of those newspaper accounts, which varied from one another, are as follows:

At around five o'clock, the professor was seen in Hartford by Brown Taylor, who was passing through town headed toward Geneva. Taylor called out to Avant, but he did not acknowledge the call. Professor Avant was also seen by a black man, Frank Martin, a resident of Slocomb, who was in a car with another black man just outside the Hartford city limits shortly after 5:00 p.m., headed toward Geneva ("Posse Scouring Countryside for Missing Teacher: Citizens in 15 Cars, Fearing Foul Play, Institute Search for Prof. Avant," *Dothan [AL] Eagle*, September 25, 1928, 1; "Numerous Theories Advanced in Effort to Solve Murder Mystery," *Dothan [AL] Eagle*, October 3, 1928, 3).

There was evidence at the site where Professor Avant's body had been found that a vehicle had collided with a stump with some force. However, the axle of the professor's car was not found to be bent. The axle of the car driven by Frank Martin and the other black man was bent, and neither was able to account for his whereabouts on Sunday afternoon during Professor Avant's disappearance and murder. A newspaper article stated that both black men were husky and exceptionally powerful men. Martin and the other black man subsequently were taken into custody on a blanket charge ("Posse Scouring Countryside"; "Numerous Theories Advanced").

A third witness, Pearl Moss, saw Professor Avant's empty car at about 7:00 p.m. as she was walking with her friend, Thurman West, through the school campus on a shortcut to the house where she boarded. She stated that she could not be certain that the car was Professor Avant's but that a Ford coupe appearing to be his was parked at the rear door of the schoolhouse near the chemical laboratory. No one was visible in the car, and there were no lights on in the car or in the schoolhouse ("Numerous Theories Advanced").

The same Ford coupe, or a similar one, passed her boarding house a few minutes after she arrived there, heading down the road toward Noma, Florida, on the same road used to travel to Bonifay. She stated that there was only one person in the car. Pearl Moss's friend, Thurman West, was later taken into custody and held in the Geneva County Jail as a suspect but was later released ("Numerous Theories Advanced").

A resident living near the One Mile Well on the Choctawhatchee River near Geneva said that he saw a Ford coupe drive up to the well on Sunday just before dark. The car was occupied by three men, one wearing a "mackinaw" (a rain-coat) and two wearing caps. Another person (who it can only be presumed was Professor Avant) was in between the two men wearing caps, and his head was covered with a flour sack. The witness stated that the man in the "mackinaw" got out of the car, looked around for a few minutes, and then got back in the car and drove off ("Numerous Theories Advanced").

Another witness, who was driving behind the coupe, substantiated the above story. Both cars stopped on a bridge and the man in the "mackinaw" got out, but when he saw the other car, he got back in and drove off toward Bonifay ("Numerous Theories Advanced").

A similar account was printed in "The Knife," where it was stated that on the Sunday night that the professor disappeared, a resident of Coffee County by the name of Wiley Gatlin, who was living near Elba, Alabama, became lost on a Geneva road. He had stopped frequently to wipe the rain from his windshield, and once while stopped he had encountered two cars passing him by. He witnessed the second car run into the back of the lead car, and he saw both cars stop. Gatlin approached the second car and asked if the occupants needed assistance. One of the men responded that they weren't in any trouble and that they were transporting a sick man to the hospital. Gatlin said that he saw the figure of a man wrapped in a blanket slouched forward on the seat of the lead car. Assuming everything was all right, Gatlin got back in his car and proceeded on his way home (Stephens).

There was a report that a man named Coley Wilson, who lived with his father in the area where the professor's car was found, saw a light shining through the trees on the Sunday night that Professor Avant had disappeared at around 9:30 p.m. However, he didn't think anything of it because he assumed it was coming from a campfire (Stephens).

It was reported by C. W. Simmons of Dundee, a small town near Hartford, that he saw Charlie Brown (the same Charlie Brown who later was indicted) wearing a new gray hat and when he questioned Brown, he said that the professor had given him the hat. This, it seemed, was suspicious because a schoolboy who had passed through the hallway of the school building on the Sunday afternoon that the professor had disappeared stated that he had seen the hat on the seat of Professor Avant's car upon emerging from the school. He said that the car was parked near the curb and that the hat was resting on the car's seat. The professor often worked late in the afternoons and evenings, and he was known to leave his hat on his car seat. The description of the hat given by Simmons matched that of the hat that Brown was seen wearing. Because Brown had previously testified to having seen the professor on the Hartford road in a "dazed" condition, he was considered a suspect and was arrested and questioned. But Brown maintained his innocence, adhering to his story that Avant had given him the hat quite a while prior to his disappearance. Brown's belongings were searched, and the hat, mysteriously, was never found. Thus he was released as a suspect (Stephens).

An illiterate cotton picker by the name of Jim Dunlap confessed in fairly legible handwriting to the Avant murder, but the confession later was refuted. Dunlap claimed that he and his boss, Gillis Bracewell, had murdered Professor Avant. A newspaper account claims that both Dunlap and Bracewell were slim and did not appear to be very strong—unlike Frank Martin and his cohort, mentioned previously, whose car bumper was bent and who had been taken into custody—and that even though Bracewell was the stronger of the two, he was of slight build (Stephens).

Nineteen-year-old George Grice of Slocomb, who had attended Slocomb High School and who had confessed a few years earlier to setting the school on fire, was arrested on Sunday morning and held in jail for questioning. He was said to have ridden by car with Thurman West and two black men to Hartford on the Sunday afternoon of Professor Avant's disappearance, arriving back in Slocomb just before dark. It was raining heavily. However, he later was released (Stephens; "Posse Scouring Countryside"; "Numerous Theories Advanced").

After the release of the above suspects, Robert H. Knowles of Moulton, Alabama, was taken into custody at the end of February 1929 while asleep at a Salvation Army refuge home and held in the Birmingham, Alabama, jail, in connection with the slaying. Attorney General McCall, who had completed a personal investigation at the scene of the crime, was expected to travel to Birmingham to question Knowles in connection with the murder. Knowles was a former principal of a school in Lamar, Alabama, in Randolph County. He had also taught school five miles from Hartford, where several of Professor Avant's relatives lived. He left there and moved to the northern part of Alabama after he and some Geneva County board of education members had a difference of opinion. Knowles, too, would later be released (Stephens).

One of the things that continued to perplex the investigators was that Professor Avant's upper torso had been bared prior to the knife being thrust into his heart. There was virtually no evidence of blood or bloodstains on his body or clothing, except for a small amount that had accumulated at the professor's waistline. The investigators concluded from this that whoever murdered the professor knew it would be highly inadvisable to leave any telltale signs of blood, which would be prime evidence in the case. The investigation team also determined that the crime had been committed by some person or persons known in the community. Finally, the team determined that this was not an ordinary crime but rather one that required extraordinary skill and expertise. Thus they were not persuaded by the theory that the professor was murdered by tramps, and they continued to pursue their theory that the perpetrator or perpetrators were familiar to Slocomb (Stephens).

Professor Avant was a man of excellent character whom everyone loved. He was well-known not only throughout Slocomb but also in Brundidge, Troy, and Hartford, Alabama. No one, including the investigation team, could figure out why anyone would want him dead.

Finally, in October 1929, the big break in the case came. The below excerpt from "The Knife" warrants reprinting in its entirety, as it adds immensely to our story and beautifully captures Phillips's character. The excerpt is reprinted in its original form without any editorial corrections or commentary (Stephens).

> In October, 1929, Lee Philips was arrested on a charge of manslaughter. He had killed man while driving a car when intoxicated. He was given a prison term of six months for the offense and transferred to the state prison in Montgomery, Alabama to begin serving his sentence. During his journey to Montgomery—impelled by what impulse no one will ever know Philips told the transfer agent, C. C. O'Bryant that he had an important statement to make to Attorney General Charlie C. McCall. It concerned, he said, the Avant murder mystery.
>
> At that time the Attorney General was in Northern Alabama and when he received word of Philips statement, he wired G. K. Fountain the prison warden to get Philips story in affidavit form. A few days later the newspapers flared forth with the startling headlines that Lee Philips had signed a partial confession in which he implicated a prominent citizen of Slocomb.
>
> The report was electrifying. A "prominent citizen!" Who could it be? And why if he was accused of the crime had his name not been made public? And why too had he not been arrested?
>
> Several days went by with no action being taken and the delay caused such fierce indignation among the citizens of Slocomb and its outlying districts that on November 1st, 1929 a mass meeting was held which was attended by more than two thousand of our townspeople. Feeling was intense and resolutions were formed demanding that the slayers of Claud Avant be brought to trial. Copies of these resolutions were sent to our circuit solicitor, to Governor Bibb Graves, and to the press. Our citizens had reached a point where silence and delay would no longer be tolerated.
>
> The Attorney General finally made a special trip to Montgomery to see Philips and get his story and, in the room where the interview took place were prison guards, a court reporter, W. J. Purvis and several others. Philips walked to a corner where he stood facing the wall his hands clasped behind him, his head bowed.

*"If you're ready to talk now Philips", McCall said quietly, "I'm here to listen, If not, I'll go."*

*Philips turned about his face looking grimly determined.*

*"I'll talk General," he said hoarsely, "Four men killed Avant for I looked in the schoolhouse winder an I see 'em do it."*

*"Who were they?" the Attorney General demanded sharply.*

*Philips gulped a little as he made his reply.*

*"They was Dr. G. W. Smith," he answered. "and Clyde Smith, his son, and Randal Jones, and Charlie Brown!*

*Dr. G. W. Smith! The effect of Phillips' statement upon his listeners was like a bombshell. Dr. Smith, one of the most respected citizens of Slocomb, with whom Claud Avant Boarded? It seemed incredible. No less incredible was the accusation of Clyde Smith, who, like his father bore and exemplary reputation. Randall Jones and Charlie Brown had both on the other hand, been at one time suspects, but the Smiths had never been under even remote suspicion of the crime. What did it mean? What motive, if Lee Philips story were true could Dr. Smith have had for seeking Claud Avant's death?*

*His hearers stared in silence at the speaker for a moment scarcely able to credit their own ears. Then the attorney General played an ace card.*

*"You didn't look in the window Philips," McCall said firmly, "The windows of the schoolhouse are to high from the ground. No when you saw that murder committed you were right in the room itself. Now tell me the truth!"*

*Again Philips turned his back on his inquisitor pacing the floor then crossing to another corner where he again faced the wall with bowed head. Then after an interval of painful silence the calm that had possessed the prisoner up to now gave way to an impetuous outburst Philips faced about and spoke rapidly.*

*"Dr. Smith planned the murder," he blurted, "He said he owed Avant money and Avant was hounding him for it. So he hired Charlie Brown and Randal Jones and me to help him. His son, Clyde, helped too. I was to get three hundred dollars for my part in it, but so help me Bob, he ain't never paid me no more than three dollars!"*

*Philips paused. His listeners thought that, if his statement were true, the Doctor's failure to pay may have had something to do with the confession they were now hearing. The man continued to speak quickly and impulsively as though he was at last telling something it was a relife for him to tell.*

*"We all met Sunday night at the school," Philips declared. "It was about seven o'clock. I parked my car at Jernigan's pasture gate and walked to the school building where I found Clyde, Randall and Charlie hid behind the corner. Then Dr. Smith came up and told me I was a little late. With that he*

handed me a hammer to hit Avant with, and said we'd find him in the school office, workin' over some papers. Then him and me walked up the hall, and Clyde and Randall and Charlie, they followed us soft-like.

"When Dr. Smith and me got to the office, sure enough we saw Avant sitting there at his desk. He seen us and asked us to come in, but the Doctor said we only wanted him to help us with some figgering we'd disagreed about. Avant said he'd be glad to help us and he took the paper Dr. Smith give him and bent down to look at it. I'd been holding the hammer behind me and when Avant bent over Dr. Smith nodded for me to hit him. I hit him on the right side of the head and he hollered and fell over on his side.

"Just then Charlie, Randall and Clyde come in and Charlie had a blanket that he put on the floor. They laid Avant on it and then I see Clyde Smith jerk open the Professor's shirt front, and the Doctor bend down with a knife and stab Avant in the heart. Soon as he done this the Doctor took a syringe out of his pocket quick and pumped a yellowish stuff in the place where he'd stabbed him. I ask the Doctor next morning when I went to Slocomb why he'd pumped that stuff into Avant's heart, and he said it was to keep from bleeding and smelling to much.

"After that, we wrapped the body in the blanket, and Charlie takes his head and shoulders while Clyde and Randall takes him by the legs. They put him in Avant's coupe that was just back of the school building and then Charlie and Randall got in with the body and Clyde and me follered in the Chevrolet. Dr. Smith didn't go with us when we left the school house. It was then about seven-thirty and he said he was goin' down to Tom Jones's who was sick."

"What did you do with the hammer with which you struck Avant?" the Attorney General interrupted.

"I give it back to Dr. Smith," Philips answered promptly. "I guess maybe he put it in the car we burnt"

The hammer found in the burned Ford coupe was hereupon produced, and Philips identified it as the one with which he struck Avant. He then continued with his gruesome recital.

"Dr. Smith told us to take the body to a lake in Florida, but we had car trouble on the way and didn't go that far. Five or six miles from Bonifay we turned off on an old trail until we come to a millpond where we stopped the cars and all of us got out. Charlie grabbed Avant around the shoulders and I grabbed him around the waist and Clyde took his feet. Then we toted him across a slough and laid him down. The body was still wrapped in the blanket but Charlie pulled the blanket away and went back and throwed it in Avant's coupe.

*"Clyde Smith had some gasoline in a can and he give this to Randall: then Charlie and Randall pushed the coupe in a hollow and poured the gasoline on to it. After that they struck a match to it and then come and jumped in the car with me and Clyde, and we drove off in a hurry up the trail and come into Slocomb through Esto, Florida.*

*Philips paused in his confession wiping his forehead nervously and wetting his lips, while his listeners stood silent and appalled at the cold brutality of his narrative.*

*"When we got back to Slocomb," he at last went on, "Clyde got out in front of the lights of the car to see if there was any blood on his clothes. Then he turned to us and said the one who told about it would go like Avant did. Charlie said he'd never tell and Randall said he wouldn't neither. I went on then and got in my car and drove home about eleven-thirty but I couldn't sleep and that night"* (Stephens).

Phillips's testimony was substantiated in part by Miss Abbie Yates, the nurse in charge at the hospital and a witness at Phillips's inquisition who testified that Dr. Smith indeed had visited Tom Jones on the night of the murder—notwithstanding the fact that Dr. Smith said that he did not go out that night—and that she had noticed a spot on his shirt. She stated later that she had presumed the spot to be blood, which he had gotten while on another case. She said that the doctor continually tried to hide the spot by pulling his coat over it. However, the spot more than likely was a result of the doctor having plunged the pocketknife into Professor Avant's heart after Lee Phillips had bludgeoned him with the hammer to knock him unconscious (Stephens).

It was not until one month after Phillips's confession that Attorney General McCall finally started to move quickly on the case, and on November 25, 1929, fourteen months after the murder, the grand jury finally convened. Appearing before the grand jury were Lee Phillips, Mrs. Phillips, and some other witnesses. All five defendants were indicted for the murder, to the understandable sensation and relief of the townspeople. Both Dr. Smith and his son Clyde blatantly declared their innocence and carried on as though nothing had happened. Held in the same prison cell, they conversed with one another about everyday topics as though each day were just another day and as though nothing out of the ordinary had happened (Stephens).

All of the defendants except Phillips were released on bail on December 21, 1929, when the Alabama Court of Appeals affirmed the decision of Circuit Judge H. A. Pearce of Geneva. There was no bail set for Phillips, as he was still being held in Kilby Prison on the manslaughter charge. Dr. Smith and his son Clyde each were granted bail in the amount of two thousand dollars; Randall Jones's bail was set at one thousand dollars and Brown's was set at five hundred dollars (Stephens).

What could have possessed these men to do what they did? Who were these men who lived normal, everyday lives and among whom Slocomb's citizens felt secure and comfortable? Let's take a look at their backgrounds.

Cornelius Clyde Smith (more commonly known as Clyde Smith) was born on March 20, 1895. As a young man, he owned a machine shop. According to the 1920 U.S. Census, at age twenty-four, Clyde was the manager of a lumber mill and was married to Madge at the time, also age twenty-four. They had two children, Elizabeth, age three (who would later become a Slocomb schoolteacher), and Myra, age one.

The son of Billy Newton worked for Clyde Smith, and Clyde was very caring toward him. Clyde owned a vast amount of property in Slocomb and provided lumber and material to have a Methodist church built in Alabama on the Florida state line in memory of his parents (Tony Kelly, Max Kelly, and Don Sasser, interview by Eudon Holland, August 30, 2010, Dothan, AL).

The 1930 U.S. Census states that at age thirty-five, Clyde was the proprietor of a sawmill and his wife, Madge, worked as a schoolteacher. At that time, they had five children, four daughters (Elizabeth, age thirteen; Myra, age eleven; Sara, age nine; and Marzora, age six) and a son, Charles C., age four. They also had six boarders living with them: Jim B. Gibson, age twenty-eight, a teacher; Barney Bloomfield, age twenty-five, the proprietor of a dry goods store; Willie J. Faircloth, age twenty-three, a teacher; Elina N. Olive, age twenty-one, a teacher; Virginia Espcy, age twenty-one, a teacher; and Milton A. Kay, age twenty-two, a teacher.

Cornelius Clyde Smith died on May 23, 1971, in Dothan, Alabama. He was seventy-six at the time of his death.

Charlie Brown was a black man born about 1899. At age twenty-one, in 1920, he lived in Slocomb and worked as a farmhand. Later, in the 1930s, he also worked for Clyde Smith as a truck driver when he had his machine shop, and he continued to work for Clyde until he died (Kelly, Kelly, and Sasser interview).

Not much more is known about Lee Phillips, and virtually nothing is known about Randall Jones.

But more shocking news was about to break in the case. In December 1929, not even a month after the grand jury had convened, Lee Phillips retracted his written confession taken by the prison warden in October of 1929, claiming that he had been coerced into making the statements that he had made. Apparently Mrs. Phillips retracted her testimony as well. Upon investigation, Governor Bibb Graves found the denials to be totally untrue, and thus no credit was given to them (Stephens).

But the boat was to be further rocked when, on January 24, 1930, Mrs. Phillips made a surprise return to Montgomery, where Lee Phillips was still serving his prison sentence in Kilby Prison, and signed an affidavit retracting her previous denial. In her affidavit she alleged that both of the Smiths begged her to change her original story and told her that if she would recant it they would see to it that Lee Phillips would be pardoned. She claimed that she had no food or clothing and that the Smiths had promised that they would take care of her needs until her husband was released from prison. However, she had reconsidered and was returning to reconfirm her original testimony so that her mind could be at peace (Stephens).

On that same day, Lee Phillips also signed an affidavit affirming his original written confession, claiming that the reason he subsequently denied his testimony was that a fellow prisoner told him that he in effect was sending himself to the electric chair by confessing to his part in the murder. However, he, like his wife, had decided to come clean (Stephens).

Of interest is the fact that one newspaper account states that because Phillips was the key witness, and because he was incarcerated, trial of the case was delayed. Why Phillips's incarceration should have delayed the trial is curious, since today when a prisoner is scheduled for a hearing or a trial, he is simply brought into the court in shackles from wherever he is being held. If anything, it would seem that it would have made things more convenient since the prison deputies would simply transport him by order of the court to the courthouse, where he could be held in that jail while the trial was taking place. It would seem that the fact that he was already incarcerated on another charge should have had no bearing on his being tried for the Avant murder, and it certainly should not have delayed the murder trial ("Supreme Court to Hear Appeal: John J. Haynes and William P. Cobb to Represent State in Smith Case," *Dothan [AL] Eagle*, December 18, 1929, 1).

On and on the case dragged, and then to everyone's shock, on the Sunday morning of January 27, 1930, the front pages of the Dothan papers were plastered with the news that Dr. Smith would never face charges for the murder of Professor Avant. The reason reported was that Dr. Smith had died suddenly (and some felt conveniently) in his bed at 12:30 a.m. of a heart attack. The doctor's death, as "The Knife" stated, "robbed the legal stage of its principal actor." More on this later, as it was speculated that Dr. Smith did not die but actually staged his own death and fled the scene ("Dr. G. W. Smith Dies Suddenly Sunday Morning: Grim Reaper Claims Physician Accused of Slaying Claude Avant Months Ago," *Dothan [AL] Eagle*, January 27, 1930, 1; Stephens).

On June 3, 1930, the four remaining defendants in Claud Avant's murder trial—Lee Phillips, Clyde Smith, Randall Jones, and Charlie Brown—were indicted and entered not guilty pleas in circuit court. The four defendants faced the death sentence for the charge of first-degree murder. Not surprisingly, Lee Phillips again had denied his confession ("Not Guilty Is Plea of Avant Defendants: Four Are Arraigned at Geneva Yesterday; All Have Same Plea; State Will Ask for Death Sentence," *Dothan [AL] Eagle*, June 4, 1930, 1; Stephens).

On June 9, 1930, the trial of Lee Phillips began in the Geneva County Court House, as the state decided to try him separately from the other three. A pool of jurors had been drawn, consisting of one hundred names, and the jurors were selected from that pool. Other cases were delayed for trial until the week of June 16. Finally the case was moving ("Not Guilty Is Plea"; Stephens).

It took an entire day to select a jury from a special venue. The jurors were all men: Henry T. Gillis, W. N. Morris, Nathaniel Pridgen, Perry Green, Ezell Horn, Fletcher Cheshire, Homer Metcalf, Clarence Jorday, John F. Lake, Enos J. Vanlandingham, Reuben Thompson, and Noah Spears ("Orderly Conduct Prevails through Third Day of Phillips Trial," *Geneva County [AL] Reaper*, June 13, 1930, 1).

The all-male jury was not unusual for the times. Although women could vote by then, there were ways to prevent them from voting, and it was done by the imposition of a poll tax, which was primarily a means of preventing blacks from voting. In addition to paying a poll tax, a person had to be a property owner in order to vote. The juror list was taken from the list of property owners, which would have precluded most women from participating on a jury since the vast majority of them would not have owned property at that time.

The prosecution included Charles C. McCall, attorney general; John Haynes; J. N. Mullins, circuit solicitor; Rob. S. Ward; and G. A. Ward. Phillips was represented by the firm of Carmichael and Tiller of Geneva ("Orderly Conduct Prevails").

Among the state's witnesses was Professor Avant's brother, who identified the clothing worn by the professor, as well as his personal effects. Also testifying was W. W. Pitts, who, according to one newspaper, found the body near the end of a mill dam near his home, although this conflicts with "The Knife," which states that it was J. D. Davis who found the body. Mrs. Rush Hinson, who lived near Slocomb High School, testified that she had heard a distressed cry—presumably the cry of Professor Avant—on the night of the murder ("Orderly Conduct Prevails"; Stephens).

It was reported that Lee Phillips, wearing tennis shoes, an orange shirt, and dark trousers, sat quietly during the trial, which moved along at a steady speed. He chewed gum and only periodically showed signs of nervousness ("Orderly Conduct Prevails"; Stephens).

After seven days, the trial came to a close, and when the Geneva County

Circuit Court jury began deliberating over the evidence presented in the case, there was already speculation that there might be a mistrial. The day was dark, cloudy, and misty, and the courtroom was filled with fifty to seventy-five people when the not-guilty verdict came down on Sunday, June 15 ("Seven-Day Trial Ends with Acquittal for Phillips," *Geneva County [AL] Reaper*, June 20, 1930, 1).

The following day, Monday, the cases against Clyde Smith, Randall Jones, and Charlie Brown were declared *nolle prosequi*, and the three were given their freedom. The term *nolle prosequi* is Latin and is a legal term for "we shall no longer prosecute," which is a declaration made to the judge by a prosecutor in a criminal case, either before or during trial, meaning that the case against the defendant is being dropped. It is an admission that the charges cannot be proven, that evidence has demonstrated either innocence or a fatal flaw in the prosecution's claim, or that the district attorney has become convinced the accused is innocent. Usage of the term is rare (Tony M. Kelly, undated note to Eudon Holland).

Notwithstanding the fact that Phillips previously had confessed to his part in the murder during the initial inquisition and had repeated his testimony at his confession before the attorney general while incarcerated in Kilby Prison, at his trial he claimed he was innocent and had provided an alibi. His defense maintained that Claud Avant had been in the company of two strange men, and not Phillips, when he went missing ("Seven-Day Trial Ends"; "Geneva County Jury Debating Phillips Case: Avant Murder Trial Comes to Close Saturday Afternoon," *Anniston Star*, June 15, 1930).

The state had attempted to introduce evidence regarding the hammer that was found in Claud Avant's car at the time the body was discovered. Phillips's counsel voiced strong objections to the introduction of this evidence, and it was rendered inadmissible on the grounds that the hammer had never been identified as the one that had struck the professor, and therefore under the rules of evidence it was inadmissible. It was even too late at this point for the state to introduce scientific evidence regarding the hammer. The state then rested its case ("Seven-Day Trial Ends").

This is remarkable since the establishment of a chain of evidence is a key element in any murder case, or in any case, for that matter. Even a novice knows this, and a slip-up of this nature may have cost the prosecution its case. These were not recent law school graduates trying this case. How could a key element such as this have been overlooked in trying this case?

According to one newspaper source, the jury was instructed to exclude from its deliberations testimony from Mrs. Alex Smith to the effect that on the Monday following the night the body was found, she had seen another car pass her home going toward the Swindle Mill. It is unclear as to why the jury was instructed to disregard this testimony ("Seven-Day Trial Ends").

The defense, utilizing their tactic of attempting to divert focus from what had really happened, relied heavily on testimony as to the presence of the two tramps who were on the Slocomb-Geneva road on the afternoon that Professor Avant disappeared, diverting the focus from Phillips to these two tramps. The defense called several witnesses to the stand to testify in this regard. Although there was varying testimony as to the appearance of the tramps and their clothing, the defense seemed to be gaining ground at this stage of the trial ("Seven-Day Trial Ends").

The defense also relied on testimony regarding Claud Avant being seen driving in his car along the Slocomb-Geneva road on the Sunday of his disappearance, supposedly in an effort to make it appear that the professor had driven off on his own and to deflect the focus from those who had murdered him and then had apprehended and dumped his body ("Seven-Day Trial Ends").

Throughout the trial, the defense attorneys seemed to have attempted to mud-dy the waters. The newspapers contain several accounts of the defense attorneys focusing on alibis for Randall Jones, Clyde Smith, and Charlie Brown, although it is unclear as to why they were doing this since those three were not on trial. Counsel for Phillips attempted to create an alibi for Randall Jones by calling to the stand T. B. Hembey. Although the state objected to Hembey's testimony, the objections were overruled. Hembey provided a detailed alibi for Jones, claiming to have been with him for several hours on the afternoon of the murder. Mrs. Colie Peters was the next witness for the defense. She substantiated Hembey's testimony ("Seven-Day Trial Ends").

Next, testimony was taken from Misses Marley Faircloth and Niva Olive, teachers who had worked with Professor Avant at the time of his death and who boarded with Clyde Smith. They testified that Smith was at home at the time of Professor Avant's disappearance and that, to the best of their knowledge, he did not leave home at all that evening. Miss Marley testified further that at the time of Professor Avant's murder, Dr. Smith did not wear a mustache ("Seven-Day Trial Ends").

Phillips's attorneys then attempted to establish whether or not Dr. Smith wore a mustache at the time of the murder—another defense tactic used to throw off the focus of the case. A previous witness, M. M. Cumbie, had testified that he had met two cars on the Esto road below Slocomb and that he had recognized the driver of the first car as being Dr. Smith. He stated that he recognized Dr. Smith by his mustache ("Seven-Day Trial Ends").

Next to take the stand was Mrs. Clyde Smith, who established an alibi for her husband, stating that Clyde had been at home on the night Professor Avant was murdered and that he did not leave home at any time during that night. Clyde Smith's brother-in-law, R. J. Weatherly, substantiated Mrs. Smith's testimony

("Seven-Day Trial Ends").

Eleven blacks gave alibis for Charlie Brown, claiming they had all seen him at a wedding on the night of the murder and giving elaborate details about everything that had taken place there ("Seven-Day Trial Ends").

The defense then called a state witness, Charlie Elmore, to the stand. Elmore had previously testified that Phillips had confessed to him all of the details of the murder and had told him the parts that Dr. Smith, Clyde Smith, Randall Jones, and Charlie Brown had played in the murder. When the defense failed to get Elmore to recant his testimony, they attempted to impeach his testimony. They introduced testimony of Elmore's father, W. A. Elmore, who had testified that Charlie had said that he did not know anything about the Avant murder and that his son was testifying as a result of being solicited by Clarence May and Dr. Purvis, an undercover agent on the case. Then the defense called Clyde Smith, Randall Jones, and Charlie Brown to the stand. Each denied any part in the murder and gave alibis ("Seven-Day Trial Ends").

Lee Phillips took the stand as the last witness. He vehemently denied every charge against him and denied ever having anything to do with Professor Avant. He denied ever having gone near Slocomb High School or having been on the road to the school. He denied having talked about the case while in Kilby Prison. He stated that he was at home in bed on the night of the murder and that he did not wake up until the next morning. When cross-examined, he testified that he never went to A. H. Register's home near Slocomb on the night of the murder between eleven and twelve o'clock and offered Register a drink of whiskey, and denied that he had gone a few days later to Register and asked him not to mention anything about the visit. The defense, having presented a concrete and convincing case, rested ("Seven-Day Trial Ends").

The state submitted rebuttal testimony, offering evidence that Dr. Smith had been, in fact, wearing a mustache at the time of Professor Avant's murder. Witnesses, including Jack Davis, a barber, testified to the fact ("Seven-Day Trial Ends").

The newspapers reported that it was at this point that the most exciting part of the trial occurred, when Attorney General McCall called A. H. Register to the stand. Register testified that Phillips did in fact go to his house on the Sunday night of Professor Avant's murder between eleven o'clock and midnight and told Register that he had been to see a girl, and he offered Register a drink of liquor. He corroborated previous testimony that Phillips returned a few days later and asked Register not to mention the visit.

The defense, on cross-examination, asked Register if he at one time had not offered his testimony as a defense witness, which Register denied. He also was accused of saying to the defense attorneys previously that "a good witness always lies behind his lawyer's back." Register denied having made the statement. When Attorney General McCall jumped to his feet and began to question Register, asking him whether he had been intimidated into testifying for the defense, Register admitted, in the presence of Mr. Tiller, Mr. Carmichael, and Foster Smith, to having been intimidated, at which point the crowd in the courtroom erupted into cheers. Judge Pearce ordered the courtroom cleared, and the defense attempted to impeach Register's testimony by bringing Foster Smith to the stand. The state objected on the grounds that Smith, who had been in the courtroom, had heard Register's testimony, and the objection was sustained. Judge Pearce called a recess until Saturday morning ("Seven-Day Trial Ends").

A. A. Carmichael, one of Phillips's attorneys, was called to the stand on Saturday morning as a rebuttal witness to rebut Register's testimony. When all of the evidence for the state and the defense had been presented, both sides rested (Stephens).

In his opening argument to the jury, Attorney General McCall asked the jurors to find Phillips guilty and to request death by the electric chair. The defense's opening argument was presented by A. A. Carmichael and H. G. Tiller. The state's closing argument was presented by Solicitor J. N. Mullins, who again asked for the death penalty for Phillips, which brought the crowded courtroom to tears. It must have been a huge relief for those in the courtroom to know that justice finally was being served. Judge Pearce charged the jury, and after about twenty-two hours of deliberation, the jurors returned their verdict of not guilty ("Seven-Day Trial Ends").

Several questions are raised by the outcome of the trial. Many believe the case was decided even before it went to the jury. Some believe the defense knew who the jurors were before the trial started. And one thing is for certain: With Lee Phillips off the hook, there was no way that Clyde Smith, Randall Jones, and Charlie Brown were going to be tried (Kelly, Kelly, and Sasser interview).

The attorney general's case seems to have been weak. Was he merely incompetent, or was he unprepared to try Phillips? It may be that the prosecution was simply not prepared or was not adequately equipped to try the case. It seems fairly obvious that the state erred grievously in its introduction of the evidence in the case when it attempted at a late stage of the trial to introduce the hammer, the weapon used by Phillips to knock Professor Avant unconscious, which was found in the professor's car where his body was discovered. Right there, that key piece of evidence should have been carefully preserved as the first and most important piece of evidence, aside from the knife, to be presented at trial.

At Phillips's initial confession he described using the hammer to hit Professor Avant over the head to knock him unconscious before Dr. Smith stabbed him to death. Then again, when he summoned the attorney general to Kilby Prison in

Montgomery, he testified to hitting the professor over the head with the hammer at the high school on the night of September 23, 1928, and that he witnessed Clyde Smith open up the professor's shirt while Dr. Smith plunged the knife into his heart. Those facts should also have been hammered (no pun intended) into the jury by the attorney general at trial.

However, even though the hammer was identified during Phillips's confession at Kilby Prison as the one he had used to hit the professor, at the beginning of the trial, the attorney general apparently failed to preserve that key piece of evidence and to identify the hammer found at the scene as the one that Phillips used. That is something that every prosecutor would have known to do. As a result, when he later tried to introduce it, it was rendered inadmissible because it had not been identified at the outset as the hammer that had struck the professor. Customarily, this would have been done in the state's opening argument. Under the rules of evidence, then, it could not be admitted, and in effect it possibly blew the state's whole case. Was the attorney general deliberately letting Phillips off the hook, or was he inexcusably incompetent?

Also worth mentioning is the fact that Attorney General McCall continuously dragged his feet in the prosecution of the case. The investigation was repeatedly delayed, even after Dr. Smith's alleged death. Was this deliberate? Although there was every indication that this was a premeditated murder, McCall announced in one newspaper article that he had decided to wait to present the case to the grand jury until the case had been completely solved. For what reason? One might draw the conclusion that he was deliberately stalling ("Avant Case Not Abandoned by McCall, Advises: Attorney General Has Hopes of Solving Murder Mystery; He Says Today," *Dothan [AL] Eagle*, June 1, 1930, 1).

In addition, the attorney general and his investigative team should have thoroughly investigated the crime scene to search for residual material and to verify what it was. Lee Phillips described the murder scene in detail and how he had hit Professor Avant. Then he said that Dr. Smith had taken a syringe from his pocket and injected the professor with a yellowish substance at the point where he had plunged the knife into his heart to stop the bleeding and to help minimize the odor. However, the prosecution team neither investigated the scene further to determine what that substance may have been nor brought in any qualified witnesses at trial to testify regarding the yellowish substance that had been injected into the professor.

The investigative team at the initial inquest included two medical doctors, Dr. L. H. Paul and Dr. Dan S. Frasier, who conducted the medical examination at the scene of the crime. These medical doctors had determined that the cause of death was a blow to the right side of the head and a stab wound to the heart. They were specific and thorough enough to note that the stab wound was inflicted with enough force so as to sever the cartilage in half at the juncture of the rib and the sternum. But although the investigative team noted the almost complete lack of blood, apparently not much more was done at the scene, and apparently no further examination of the professor's body was made with regard to it.

Mayor Stephens did note "curious looking specks" on chairs and on some papers and a catalog after examining the principal's office. He had the chairs, papers, and catalog tested in a lab, and it was confirmed that the specks were human blood. But at that point, the investigators were still mystified and merely labeled the killing a "bloodless stabbing." Apparently no medical experts were called to testify at trial.

One wonders why the prosecution didn't use the circumstantial evidence in the case and build upon it along with the other witnesses' testimony to form a direct link to the murder, putting the pieces together to build their case, formulating it into corroborating evidence. Phillips himself testified before the trial that he, Randall Jones, and Charlie Brown assisted in transporting Claud Avant's body from Slocomb to a designated site near Bonifay, Florida—the site at which the body was later found. How many Ford coupes and Chevrolets happened to be out driving near the Alabama-Florida state line on that Sunday, that happened to have men in them, mysteriously dressed in caps and raincoats, with a man with a flour sack over his head or wrapped in a blanket, that happened to stop on the bridge, and whose driver got back in the car and drove away when he saw another vehicle behind the car?

There is the issue of Lee Phillips's own testimony and his recanting that testimony not once, but twice. His wife, too, in December 1929, recanted her previous testimony given at the grand jury investigation of her husband regarding her husband's part in the Avant murder. Then, on January 24, 1930, she recanted her previous denial, purportedly because Dr. Smith did not live up to his obligation to pay money to her and her husband if they would change their testimony and because she wanted some peace of mind. One can only imagine how the recanting of the Phillipses' testimony looked to the jury. How is one to know how to distinguish the truth after so many lies have been told? And wouldn't that corroborate the fact that Phillips could be (and probably was) lying at trial? ("Lee Phillips' Wife Claims She Lied at Avant Hearing in Geneva Last Month," *Geneva County [AL] Reaper*, December 13, 1929, 1; Stephens).

The *Geneva County Reaper* reported that when the state presented its closing rebuttal argument, requesting that the jury return a guilty verdict and that it send Lee Phillips to the electric chair, the crowded courtroom erupted into tears—presumably tears of relief that at last one of the perpetrators of this horrific crime against the town's beloved professor would be punished and that justice finally would be served. How tragic that after all that time waiting for the trial, none of the men was convicted ("Seven-Day Trial Ends").

As is the case in some prominent court cases throughout history, there will always remain questions as to whether the jury, the prosecution, or both were swayed. Perhaps even the judge was influenced. But one thing does appear to be true, and that is that murder did appear to be the safest crime of the day in Slocomb back in 1928—at least for the rich and powerful.

Although Slocomb turned a whole lot uglier and a whole lot scarier on that day in September 1928 when Claud Avant was murdered, the reality was that things had been mean and stormy for quite some time, and that things in the pretty, pristine little town were not as they appeared to be on the surface. Slocomb, like other towns in the South and in Geneva County in the late 1920s, was one rough and rugged place.

It was the era of boxing, brawls, extreme poverty, and the soon-to-come Great Depression of 1929. There were cases of townspeople being charged with public drunkenness, disorderly conduct, abuse and battery, gambling, and even adultery (it was always women—not men—who were charged as adulterers) (Harris Holmes). Prohibition, which hit Slocomb and Geneva County in 1930, was characterized by bootlegging and crime, including murder.

In 1928, Slocomb was a wild town. Neighboring Dothan was no different. In fact, that town can boast that the pages of its history include an actual shootout. In the downtown district of Dothan today there resides a mural depicting the

Mural in downtown Dothan depicting the shootout.

shootout, which erupted as a result of a proposed tax imposition on cotton wagons traveling into the downtown district in the late 1920s. One must consider the times and individual attitudes and what was or was not acceptable.

And it may not be all too surprising that someone of the stature of a medical doctor could get away with murder—or multiple murders—in a town like Slocomb during that era. It might have been quite easy for a medical doctor in those times to pull off murdering several victims by poisoning them over a period of time.

But the murder of Claud Avant was different. It was violent, brutal, and messy. It was cunningly calculated. It was orchestrated by a ringleader who had to work quickly to do away with the victim who knew too much; thus, the haste with which it was carried out.

What happened is left for us to decide. Was Dr. Smith so crafty that he was even able to get his own son to go along with a cold-blooded massacre? Throughout history, there are documented cases of those who will do anything—even lie under oath and, yes, commit murder—if the price is right.

# Chapter 5

## Dr. Smith's "Death"

Dr. Smith's third wife, Gussie (McAllister) Smith, and baby son, George Washington Smith, were among those surviving his "death," if in fact he died. (Interestingly, Dr. Smith's mother was a McAllister, and as previously noted, he and Gussie were distant cousins.) Others in his immediate family included his three other children: Clyde, Atkinson Angus of Hartford (an attorney), and Dr. Gordon Royce Smith of Ozark.

It was reported that Dr. Smith awoke in the early morning hours of Sunday, January 26, 1930, complaining to his wife that he was not feeling well. He spoke with her for a while and then asked her to turn the light out so that he could sleep. A few minutes later, according to his wife, he was making gulping sounds and she called the doctor, but he purportedly died before the doctor arrived ("Dr. G. W. Smith Dies Suddenly Sunday Morning," *Dothan [AL] Eagle*, January 27, 1930, 1).

Gussie hung around in Alabama for a while. According to the 1930 U.S. Census, she was living at 403 Adams Street in Dothan, Alabama, in Houston County, with her son, George W., and a black nurse. She was thirty-four years old and owned her own home and a radio—something significant enough in 1930 to have been listed as property on the census report. But by 1935, she had moved to Florida and was living in Chipley, in Washington County. She was head of the household, and her profession, according to the U.S. Census, was that of a nurse. Her son, George W., was six years old (Van Sickle).

In 1945, Gussie was forty-nine and was still living in Chipley. She was still a practicing nurse. George W. was fifteen years old and was in the eleventh grade (Van Sickle).

Things were wrapped up pretty quickly and tidily for a man of Dr. Smith's status and standing in Slocomb and Geneva County. Funeral services were held at 2:00 p.m. on Monday, January 27, only a day after the death, with a closed casket and with interment following in the Slocomb Pleasant Hills Cemetery. The Houston Funeral Home in Dothan handled the arrangements. Why a funeral home in another county? It seems somewhat curious. Only one doctor, Dr. Mordecai E. Doughty, saw the body ("Dr. G. W. Smith Dies Suddenly").

Dr. Smith purportedly began having similar attacks to the one that claimed his life while he was incarcerated in the Geneva County Jail. Is it possible that, being the "shrewd old cookie" that he was, he might have begun calculating and laying the groundwork for his own "funeral" even while there? ("Dr. G. W. Smith Dies Suddenly"; Mertice Mae Armstrong interview).

Newspaper reports stated that the cause of death was a heart attack of cardiac asthma, and the death certificate, signed by Dr. Doughty, confirms that fact. However, Dr. Smith was a relatively young man of fifty-eight. No autopsy was done, which may or may not be unusual but which presumably would not have been difficult or too costly with the connections that he would have had in the medical community.

What is extremely significant is the fact that pallbearers said that the closed casket just didn't feel right. There were reports that it felt like the casket contained bricks and not a human body. Other individuals have speculated that the casket contained a wax dummy. There was also speculation that there may have been someone else's body in the casket (Billy B. Newton, Tony Kelly, and others, interview by Eudon Holland, August 30, 2010, Dothan, AL; Max Kelly, Dutch Holland, and others, interview by Eudon Holland, August 27, 2010, Dothan, AL).

It was stated back in the 1930s by Dr. Stevens, Joshua Purvis (Slocomb's veterinarian), and Jim Kelly, the maternal grandfather of Billy Newton, that they would never believe that Dr. Smith's body was in that casket unless somebody lifted the casket and they saw the skeleton for themselves (Billy B. Newton, interview by Eudon Holland, September 4, 2010, Dothan, AL).

There were also rumors of sightings of Dr. Smith in Atlanta after his death, as well as a sighting in Texas by the former bookkeeper of Slocomb High School (Kelly, Holland, and others interview).

How authentic was Dr. G. W. Smith? Just how genuine and trustworthy a human being was he? The Medical Association of the State of Alabama, in reviewing Dr. Smith's credentials, ascertained that his papers were "very defective" and that he did "not seem to have merited" the M.D. certificate granted by the Louisville Medical College in 1892 ("Transactions of the Medical Association of the State of Alabama—By Medical Association of the State of Alabama"). Upon further investigation, the Johns Hopkins University website does not list among its alumni a Gordon Wright Smith. Taking things a step further, a call to the university revealed that the records contain no listing of a Gordon Wright Smith having attended the university in 1910, although the university representative did say that the records were not as accurate in those days. Would Dr. Smith, the man who swore an oath to protect and heal—the man who brought life into the world—have used his prominence and power to commit murder? Could he have conspired with his own son and have used his medical background in ways to harm and kill? Is it possible that he could have been on such a power trip that he would go so far as to stage his own death so as to avoid punishment for his crimes?

# Chapter 6

## The Case of the Missing Sewing Machine Repairman:
### The Murder of Mr. Gayles

It is said that the truth will always prevail and that evil deeds will come back to haunt the perpetrator one day. But the murderer of one poor soul whose body was never discovered seems to have eluded that theory.

State law enforcement officers directed the investigation into the missing man on a late winter day in February 1930. It was believed that he had been murdered twelve years earlier by a jealous lover and his accomplice and that his body had been dumped into a well, although his body was never found. The man, a traveling sewing machine repairman by the name of Gayles (nobody knew his first name), was said to have boarded at the home of Dr. Smith while staying in Slocomb. As the story goes, Gayles was said to have corresponded with a Slocomb lady prior to his arrival there, with the intent of marrying her. However, he disappeared mysteriously ("New Murder Mystery Existing at Slocomb," *Geneva County [AL] Reaper*, February 14, 1930).

The case would have remained unsolved and would have been buried in the annals of Slocomb's past except that the murderer's accomplice, while intoxicated, all of a sudden began foolishly bragging about his part in the dastardly deed to a fellow drinker. Investigators began to piece together key elements of the case and located the well where the body had been purportedly dumped (which by then had been filled in). A witness who allegedly saw Gayles's dead body had been discovered, and events leading up to the murder were uncovered ("New Murder Mystery Existing").

As the story began to unravel, investigators learned that Gayles had traveled to Slocomb from a northern state and had boarded temporarily with Dr. Smith and Aunt Dixie. One day, he ventured to the home of farmer B. L. Holloway and his wife, about five miles outside of Slocomb, asking if he could repair their sewing machine. Mr. Holloway said that their sewing machine did not need repairs. Mr. Gayles asked if the Holloways would give him refuge, claiming Dr. Smith was searching for him. Mr. Holloway then said that he could hide in an old stall located away from the main house.

Mr. Holloway told investigators that Dr. Smith and Bill Collins arrived at his house a short time later asking for Mr. Gayles, and he directed him to the stall since Bill Collins told him that Mr. Gayles was trying to get out of paying what he owed Dr. Smith for boarding with him. Dr. Smith and Bill Collins went to the stall, pulled Mr. Gayles out by the arm, forced him into their vehicle, and drove off with him. No one saw him after that. Contacts in the North from where Mr. Gayles had resided had written asking for information about him, but no one was able to account for his whereabouts ("New Murder Mystery Existing").

Mr. Holloway followed up with Bill Collins a few days afterward, asking what had become of Mr. Gayles, and was told that Dr. Smith, who had learned that Mr. Gayles was a Mason and of high standing, had given him some money and he had left town ("New Murder Mystery Existing").

A witness, who subsequently had moved to Florida, provided information to investigators relative to having seen two men with a dead body on the creek bridge near the well where the investigation was being conducted. As a crowd of people stood about in the cold, waiting with bated breath for what would be drawn up from the old well, an axe was lifted from about twelve feet below ground level. However, although Dr. Smith's alleged accomplice purportedly claimed to have dumped Gayles's body in the well, the skeletal remains apparently were never recovered ("New Murder Mystery Existing").

What was the nature of Mr. Gayles's travels to Slocomb? It was reported that he had corresponded with a lady prior to his arrival. It also was reported by the newspaper that carried the story of the investigation into his disappearance twelve years prior that he had gone missing as a result of a dispute with a jealous lover. The investigation into this poor man's disappearance and the search for his body began in February 1930. At that time it was reported that he had gone to Slocomb, had boarded with Dr. Smith, had been involved in the jealous lover encounter, and had gone missing twelve years before then, which would put the events in the approximate year of 1918 ("New Murder Mystery Existing").

It was in January 1918 that Theodora Atkinson Smith, Dr. Smith's first wife, died. In July 1919, Dr. Smith married Aunt Dixie, which would have put Mr. Gayles's appearance in Slocomb and his stay at Dr. Smith's house in exactly the same time frame. This could lead one to speculate that Dr. Smith may have had something to do with the murder of Mr. Gayles.

If Dr. Smith's and Gayles's paths had crossed, and if there was something going on between them and Aunt Dixie, what other love triangles might Dr. Smith have been involved in? Just what transpired under the roof of that big, beautiful house in Slocomb, Alabama, that gave such an appearance of opulence and beauty? Exactly when did Mr. Gayles arrive at the Smith house? Was it Aunt Dixie with whom he had corresponded prior to his arrival? Was it she whom he had hoped to court and marry, or did he become involved with her after his arrival? Could it be that Dr. Smith was incited to such a state of jealousy and rage that he could have been capable of the murder of this salesman? These are questions that will probably remain unanswered.

Was Dr. Smith involved in the murders mentioned in this book or in other murders? Are there other cold cases that loom in the gray shadows of the police and sheriff's stations of Slocomb and Geneva County, waiting like sealed coffins to be pried open at long last and put to rest? How many? How many skeletons lie beneath Slocomb's cold, red clay, that sleep silently engulfed by the long, choking fingers of kudzu vines? How many ghosts haunt Slocomb and Geneva County's wooded grasslands—dead, muffled cries shooting up from the earth like sparks of wiregrass, yearning to tell the world their secrets—innocent victims of the perverted vengeance of the prominent, the powerful, and the wealthy? Perhaps we will never know—or perhaps this is just the tip of an iceberg that is just beginning to emerge.

𝕰**udon** 𝕳**offand** was born in Esto, Florida, and lived in six different cities by the time he was fifteen years old, spending a good part of his childhood in Enterprise, Alabama. He attended Heidelberg College (Tiffin, OH) and graduated from Wayne State University (Detroit, MI). He formerly served as Treasurer of Northville Township, Michigan, and is a former agent for the Internal Revenue Service. An avid historian, Eudon published his memoirs, *Boiled Peanuts and Buckeyes* (Northville, MI: Ferne Press), with Laurie A. Palazzolo and Danny Kanat in 2006. Along with several other writers, he and Ms. Palazzolo are currently working on a biography about the life of one of Heidelberg College's most renowned football coaches, Paul Hoernemann. Eudon currently resides in Northville, where he works as a C.P.A. and C.F.P. and continues to be involved in the community.

𝕷aurie 𝒜. 𝕻alazzolo was born in Detroit and holds a B.S. from Madonna University (Livonia, MI) in Paralegal Studies/Business Administration, and a M.A. from Wayne State University (Detroit, MI) in English–Business, Professional and Technical Writing. She is the author of the book *Horn Man: The Polish-American Musician in Twentieth-Century Detroit*, released in October 2003 with distribution through Wayne State University Press. She has worked in the legal profession and as a researcher and analyst. She currently resides in Farmington, Michigan, where she is actively involved in the community and in Polish and Polish-American history, and where she serves on several boards.

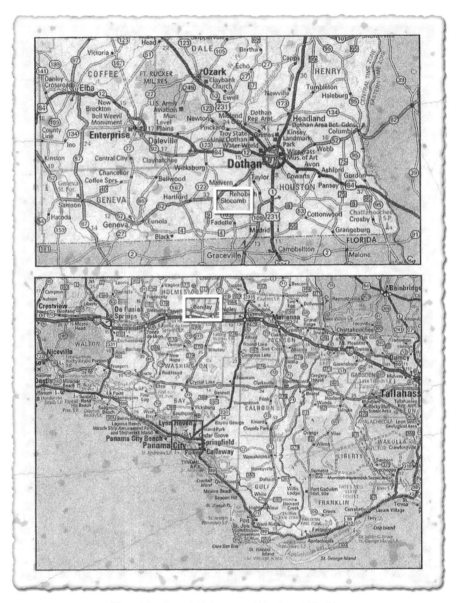

Map of Southeast Alabama and Northwest Florida.

# Sources

Armstrong, Mertice Mae. Interview by Eudon Holland. December 26, 1987.

"Auburn Freshman Discovered Dead Early This A.M." *The (Auburn, AL) Plainsman*, March 5, 1932.

"Avant Case Not Abandoned By Mccall, Advises: Attorney General Has Hopes of Solving Murder Mystery; He Says Today." *Dothan (AL) Eagle*, June 1, 1930, 1.

"Avant Case Will Not Go before Grand Jury Yet: Attorney General Charlie McCall Says Case Needs Further Investigation." *Dothan (AL) Eagle*, March 13, 1929, 1.

"Brutal Murder Slocomb, Ala., School Principal, Whose Body Was Found near Bonifay Last Friday, Remains a Complete Mystery." Unidentified newspaper clipping, October 5, 1928.

"Court Affirms the Decision of Circuit Judge: Decision on Appeal by Attorney General Is Rendered Today." *Dothan (AL) Eagle*, December 21, 1929, 1.

"Dr. G. W. Smith Dies Suddenly Sunday Morning: Grim Reaper Claims Physician Accused of Slaying Claude Avant Months Ago." *Dothan (AL) Eagle*, January 27, 1930, 1.

Everett, Lon, and James Earl Best Jr. *From Holme to Holmes: The Saga of the Whitaker Family in America*. Dothan, AL: Minuteman Press, 1991.

"Geneva County Jury Debating Phillips Case: Avant Murder Trial Comes to Close Saturday Afternoon." *Anniston Star*, June 15, 1930.

Godwin, (Mrs.) J. H. "History and Friendly Stories of Holmes County and It's [*sic*] Friendly People." *Holmes County (FL) Advertiser*, August 1, 1947, 2.

Harris, Trudier. "Sharecropping." http://www.english.illinois.edu/maps/poets/a_f/brown/sharecropping.htm.

Harris Holmes, Era Jo. *My Home Town: A History of Slocomb, Alabama: 1901–2001*. Self-published.

*The Heritage of Geneva County, Alabama*, Geneva, AL, undated.

Holland, Lee Eudon, Laurie A. Palazzolo, and Danny Kanat. *Boiled Peanuts and Buckeyes*. Northville, MI: Ferne Press, 2006.

"Indictment Is Predicted in C. F. Avant Case: McCall's Agent Says New Evidence May Lead to Speedy Grand Jury Action." *Dothan (AL) Eagle*, February 25, 1929, 1.

"J. H. Keith Gets 15 Years for Filling Station Robbery." *Geneva County (AL) Reaper*, June 13, 1930, 1.

Kelly, Max, Dutch Holland, and others. Interview by Eudon Holland, August 27, 2010, Dothan, AL.

Kelly, Tony. Interview by Eudon Holland. September 4, 2010, Dothan, AL.

Kelly, Tony. Undated note to Eudon Holland.

Kelly, Tony, Max Kelly, and Don Sasser. Interview by Eudon Holland. August 30, 2010, Dothan, AL.

"Lee Phillips Held in Geneva County Jail; Avant Case: Alleged 'Co-Murderer' Arrested after Release from Kilby Penitentiary." *Dothan (AL) Eagle*, May 1, 1930, 1.

"Lee Phillips' Wife Claims She Lied at Avant Hearing in Geneva Last Month." *Geneva County (AL) Reaper*, December 13, 1929, 1.

"Moulton Man Detained in the Avant Murder: Robert H. Knowles Held in Birmingham Jail for Questioning by McCall: Chief Detective Cole Makes Arrest Friday: Evidence Prompting Arrest Kept Secret by State Law Enforcement Men." *Dothan (AL) Eagle*, February 23, 1929, 1.

"Murder a Safe Crime." *Geneva County (AL) Reaper*, November 16, 1928.

"Negro in Kilby for Safe Keeping Today." *Dothan (AL) Eagle*, December 18, 1929, 1.

"New Murder Mystery Existing at Slocomb." *Geneva County (AL) Reaper*, February 14, 1930.

Newton, Billy B. Interview by Eudon Holland. September 4, 2010, Dothan, AL.

Newton, Billy B, Tony Kelly, Dutch Holland, and others. Interview by Eudon Holland. August 30, 2010, Dothan, AL.

"Not Guilty Is Plea of Avant Defendants: Four Are Arraigned at Geneva Yesterday; All Have Same Plea; State Will Ask for Death Sentence." *Dothan (AL) Eagle,* June 4, 1930, 1.

"Numerous Theories Advanced in Effort to Solve Murder Mystery." *Dothan (AL) Eagle*, October 3, 1928, 3.

"Orderly Conduct Prevails through Third Day of Phillips Trial." *Geneva County (AL) Reaper*, June 13, 1930, 1.

"Posse Scouring Countryside for Missing Teacher." *Dothan (AL) Eagle*, September 25, 1928, 1.

"Slocomb Man Is Carried Geneva [sic] Jail Yesterday: Officers Refuse to Talk after Finding Half Pint Liquor in Lee Phillips' Home." *Dothan (AL) Eagle*, March 12, 1929, 1.

Stephens, Mayor D. D., as told to James Cato Pattillo. "The Knife." *True Detective*.

"Supreme Court to Hear Appeal: John J. Haynes and William P. Cobb to Represent State in Smith Case." *Dothan (AL) Eagle*, December 18, 1929, 1.

"To Die in Electric Chair for Assault on Woman." Unidentified newspaper clipping, 1928.

"Transactions of the Medical Association of the State of Alabama—By Medical Association of the State of Alabama."

"Woman Goes to Pen." *Dothan (AL) Eagle*, May 27, 1930, 1.